The Complete Rock Guitar Player.

by Steve Tarshis.

Omnibus Edition.

Amsco Publications
New York/London/Sydney/Cologne

Photographs:

Book 1

Robert Matthew/Retna Ltd.	6
Michael Putland/Retna Ltd.	8, 20
Beth Gwinn/Retna Ltd.	10
Andrea Laubach/Retna Ltd.	12
David Redfern/Retna Ltd.	14, 18, 22
Janette Beckman/Retna Ltd.	16
Walter McBride/Retna Ltd.	25

Book 2

Gary Gershoff/Retna Ltd.	5
Peter Simon/Retna Ltd.	8
David Redfern/Retna Ltd.	15, 27
Joel Axelrad/Retna Ltd.	18
Michael Putland/Retna Ltd.	20
Larry Busacca/Retna Ltd.	26

Book 3

Gary Gershoff/Retna Ltd.	10
Paul Cox/Retna Ltd.	13, 17
Godlis/Retna Ltd.	22
Chris Walter/Retna Ltd.	26
Michael Putland/Retna Ltd.	29
Barry Schultz/Retna Ltd.	7
Joseph Sial/Retna Ltd.	24

Book 4

Gary Gershoff/Retna Ltd.	5
Chris Walter/Retna Ltd.	11
Larry Busacca/Retna Ltd.	15
David Redfern/Retna Ltd.	20
Michael Putland/Retna Ltd.	22, 27
Andrea Laubach/Retna Ltd.	29

Edited by Peter Pickow
Interior layout and design by Leonard Vogler
Illustrative photography by M. Butler and A. Kopp

International Standard Book Number: 0.8256.1168.7

Exclusive Distributors:
Music Sales Corporation
24 East 22nd Street, New York, NY 10010 USA
Music Sales Limited
8/9 Frith Street, London W1V 5TZ England
Music Sales Pty. Limited
120 Rothschild Street, Rosebery, Sydney, NSW 2018, Australia

Printed in the United States of America by
Vicks Lithograph and Printing Corporation

Contents

The Songs

About This Book

This is the first book of an exciting new series for the aspiring rock guitarist. You will learn from a unique perspective. Right from the beginning you will be playing some of the greatest rock songs ever written; songs made famous by the all-time greats; from Chuck Berry to the Police.

You will learn the basic material that all guitarists need to know, but you will also learn those techniques which are unique to rock music.

You can use this book on your own, in a classroom, or with a private teacher. The notation, especially at the beginning, is simple and easy to follow. The words to the songs are also included.

So here it is. With a little practice, I think you can have some fun and get a pretty good start on rock 'n' roll guitar.

Holding the Guitar

Many rock 'n' roll guitarists have developed their own styles of holding their instruments, but basically, the guitar is held as shown below.

Sitting position:

Standing position:

The right hand is used for strumming. Hold the pick between the thumb and first finger, as shown below.

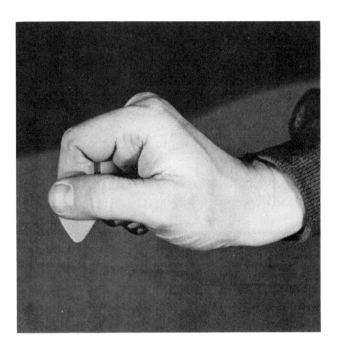

The left hand is used to press the strings of the guitar down onto the fretboard to play notes and chords.

The crook of the right arm rests on the corner of the guitar so that the forearm can strum freely. The right hand falls over the strings at the sound hold (acoustic guitar) or at the pickups (electric guitar).

The left hand should hang freely also. Try not to rest your left elbow on your knee when sitting.

Tuning the Guitar

Before each playing session, you must tune your guitar. Many guitarists use electronic tuners. These are small devices (they fit in your case) which are not too expensive. They are especially useful for electric guitars.

There is also a method known as relative tuning. With this method you tune the guitar to itself. Estimate the correct pitch of the sixth, or E, string (the lowest sounding string). Play the fifth fret of the sixth string and listen to the sound. Tune the open fifth string up or down until it matches that sound. Now play the fifth fret of the fifth string, and tune the open fourth string to that sound. Next play the fifth fret of the fourth string, and tune the open third string to that sound. Now play the third string at the fourth fret, and tune the open second string to that sound. Finally, play the fifth fret of the second string, and tune the open first string to that sound.

Parts of the Guitar

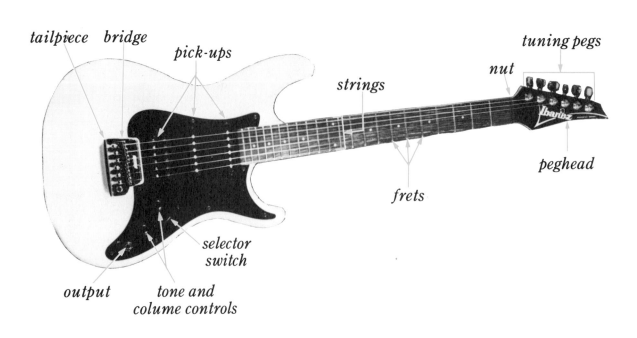

The Basic Strum

The heart of rock 'n' roll has always been the beat, and the heart of rock 'n' roll guitar is the rhythm. Without a good rhythm, even a good song can sound bad. The opposite is also true: With a good rocking rhythm, almost anything can sound good.

For a rock guitar player, the rhythm lies in the right hand, the hand that holds the pick. For this reason, the first thing we're going to work on is a right-hand strum that will always work—a "machine" that we can turn on and will always run, regardless of what the left hand is doing. For now, the left hand won't be doing anything: for this basic right-hand exercise you will be strumming the open strings.

The basic strum is a constant up-and-down motion. The pick is held between the thumb and first finger of the right hand and brushed against the strings. Try not to touch the wood of the guitar with the pick. The strings are as close as the pick gets to the guitar.

Most rock rhythms can be broken down into groups of four beats. As indicated in the notation below, play a downstroke for each number and an upstroke for the **and** after each number. Practice this strum slowly and evenly—what is important is not the speed, but the steadiness of the strum.

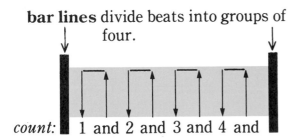

bar lines divide beats into groups of four.

count: 1 and 2 and 3 and 4 and

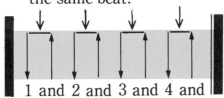

beams join strums that occur within the same beat.

1 and 2 and 3 and 4 and

Chords

In order to start making music with our basic strum, we have to learn a few chords. You can think of chords as shapes that are formed with the fingers of the left hand on the neck of the guitar. I'm going to show you how to play these shapes by using a **chord diagram.** The neck of the guitar will be shown like this:

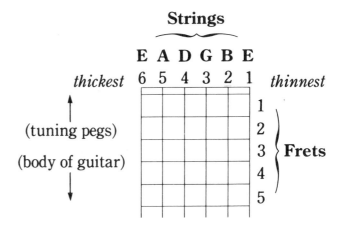

Our first chord will be **E Minor (Em).** It is played by placing the fingers of the left hand on the neck of the guitar as shown in the diagram below. The fingers of the left hand are numbered as follows:

1 = index finger
2 = middle finger
3 = ring finger
4 = pinky

Em

 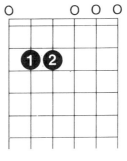

A circle indicates that the string is played open.

Miss You

When fingering a note on the guitar, position each finger as close to the metal fret bar as possible without actually touching it. (Touching the metal fret bar will give you a buzzing sound.) The diagram below shows the correct finger placement for the **Em** chord.

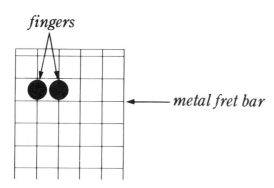

fingers

metal fret bar

Press down firmly with the first and second fingers of the left hand, and start your right-hand machine. As indicated in the notation below, strum the **Em** chord sixteen times (eight down-up motions), then strum the open strings sixteen times. Keep repeating this until you can do it smoothly. Remember, the idea is to keep the right-hand machine going, without stopping, while the left-hand fingers go on and off the neck.

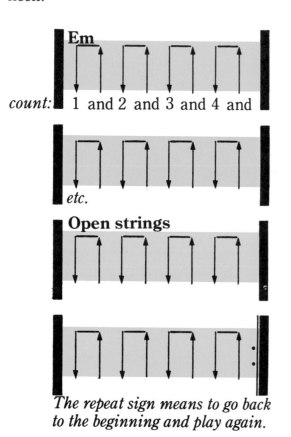

Em

count: 1 and 2 and 3 and 4 and

etc.

Open strings

The repeat sign means to go back to the beginning and play again.

With one more chord we can start playing some songs. Look at the diagram below and finger an **A Minor Seventh** chord **(Am7).**

Am7

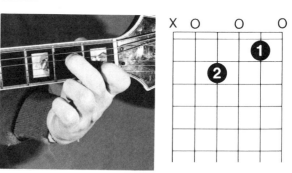

An x indicates that the string is not played.

Practice playing **Am7** using the basic strum. Then practice alternating between **Am7** and the open strings (sixteen times each). Remember, keep that right-hand machine going!

Now we're ready to play our first song, the Rolling Stones' "Miss You." To play this song we will move back and forth between **Em** and **Am7**. When switching from **Em** to **Am7**, hold the second finger down and move only the first finger. Each chord will receive sixteen strums (two groups of four beats). Each group of four beats is known as a **measure** of music.

Miss You
Words and Music by Mick Jagger and Keith Richards

Em

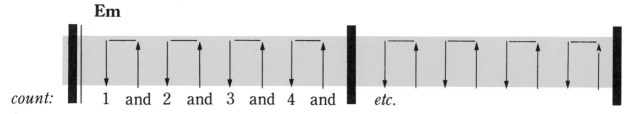

count: 1   and   2   and   3   and   4   and   *etc.*

1. I've been hold-ing out so long,___ I've been sleep-ing all a-lone.___ Girl, I
(2.) ooh ooh ooh ooh ooh,   ooh ooh   ooh ooh ooh ooh ooh,   ooh ooh

Am7

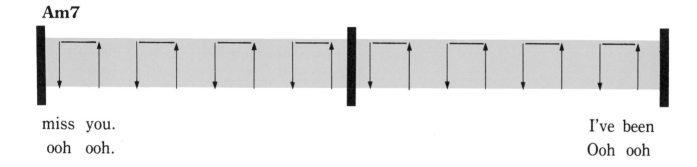

miss you.   I've been
ooh ooh.   Ooh ooh

Em

hang-ing on the phone,___ I've been sleep-ing all a-lone. I wan-na
ooh ooh ooh ooh ooh,   ooh ooh ooh ooh ooh ooh ooh, ooh ooh ooh

Am7

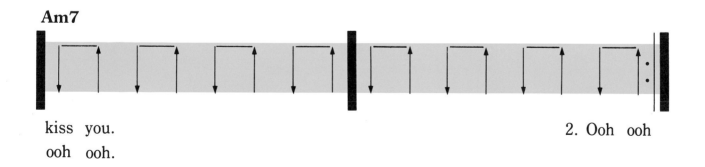

kiss you.   2. Ooh ooh
ooh ooh.

Shout

Let's learn two more chords, **C Major Seventh (Cmaj7)** and **A,** and play another song.

Cmaj7

 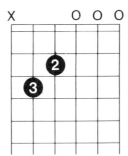

A

 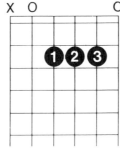

Practice these chords using the basic strum. Then practice alternating between each chord and the open strings. (Sixteen strums each) until you feel comfortable with them.

Remember, when you change chords, move only those fingers that will be on a new string or fret. For example, when moving from **Em** to **Cmaj7**, your second finger can stay where it is.

Here's another tip: When moving from **A** to **Em**, think of the first and second fingers as a unit and move them simultaneously.

Once you are ready to move the chords while strumming with the right hand, try to adopt the "machine" attitude. In other words, don't get in the habit of stopping your strumming to give yourself time to make the chord changes. Your right hand should keep going no matter what, even if the left hand is stumbling a bit. Remember, the rhythm should be your first concern when playing rock 'n' roll.

Now let's try the Tears for Fears song "Shout." Use the same down-up motion you used in "Miss You."

Shout
Words and Music by Roland Orzabel and Ian Stanley.

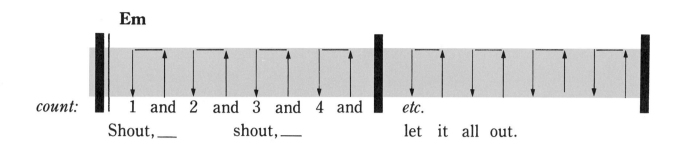

count: 1 and 2 and 3 and 4 and   *etc.*

Shout, __   shout, __   let it all out.

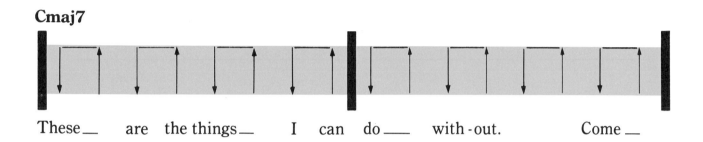

These __ are the things __ I can do __ with-out.   Come __

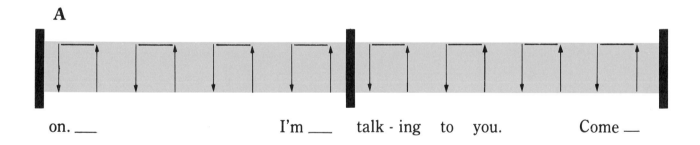

on. __   I'm __ talk - ing to you.   Come __

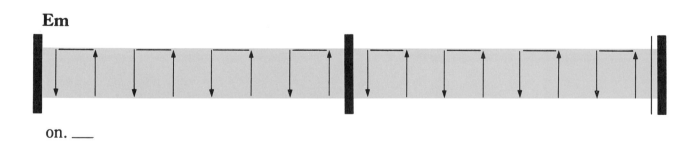

on. __

Down by the River

With the **Am7** chord and the **D7** chord we can play Neil Young's "Down by the River." First I want to show you a new strum. For this song, instead of strumming in a constant down-up, down-up pattern, we will use a down, down, down-up, down-up pattern. The important thing to realize when playing this pattern is that the first two downstrokes take up the first two full beats, or the same amount of time that two down-up strums take in the basic strum (**Strumming Pattern 1**). You can compare the two patterns in the notation below. Notice that beats three and four are the same in each pattern.

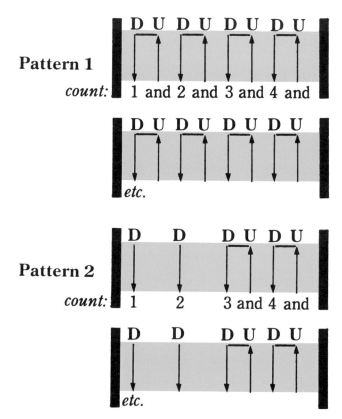

Pattern 1

count: 1 and 2 and 3 and 4 and

etc.

Pattern 2

count: 1 2 3 and 4 and

etc.

Look at the diagram below and play a D7 chord.

D7

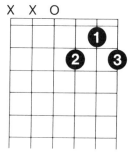

For "Down by the River," use **Strumming Pattern 2** and play one measure each of **Am7** and **D7**. Remember, when switching back and forth between **Am7** and **D7**, don't move the first finger at all. Move the other fingers in one motion, and keep the strum going no matter what!

Down by the River
Words and Music by Neil Young

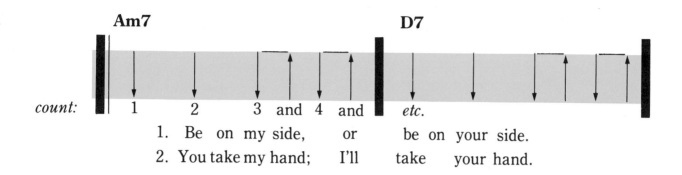

count: 1 2 3 and 4 and *etc.*

1. Be on my side, or be on your side.
2. You take my hand; I'll take your hand.

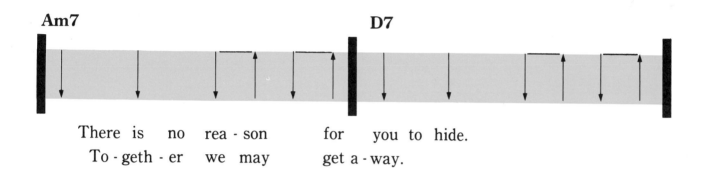

There is no rea - son for you to hide.
To - geth - er we may get a - way.

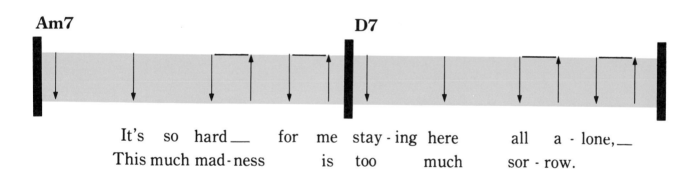

It's so hard___ for me stay - ing here all a - lone,___
This much mad - ness is too much sor - row.

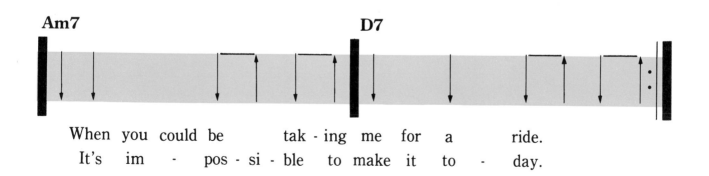

When you could be tak - ing me for a ride.
It's im - pos - si - ble to make it to - day.

From Me to You

Not let's learn two new chords so we can play a classic Beatles song, "From Me to You."

C

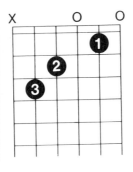

G

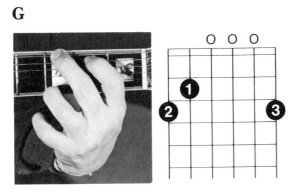

The fingering for the **C** chord is the same as the fingering for **Am7**, except that your third finger is added at the third fret of the fifth string.

Many songs that use the **C** chord also use the **G** chord. When you practice the **G** chord, make sure your left-hand fingers don't muffle the sound of the open second, third, and fourth strings. This is an important chord in rock music, so make sure it has a good, clean sound.

Use Strumming Pattern 2 to play "From Me to You."

From Me to You

Words and Music by John Lennon and Paul McCartney

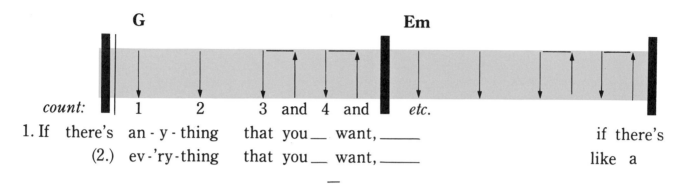

count: 1   2   3 and 4 and   *etc.*

1. If there's an-y-thing that you __ want, _____   if there's
(2.) ev-'ry-thing that you __ want, _____   like a
—

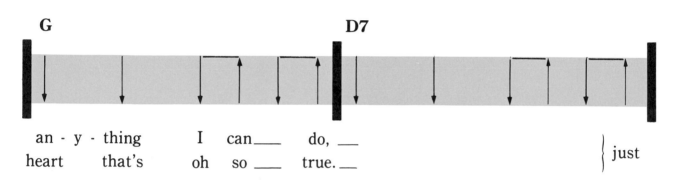

an-y-thing I can__ do, __   } just
heart that's oh so ___ true. __

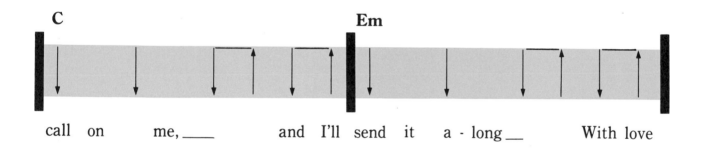

call on me, ____ and I'll send it a-long__   With love

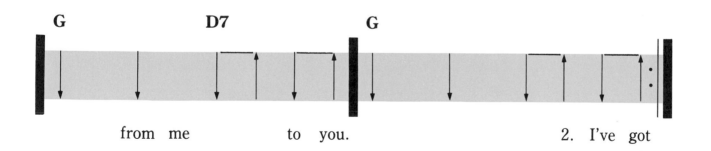

from me to you.   2. I've got

Roxanne

To play "Roxanne," by the Police, you need to learn two new chords, **D** and **Bm.**

D

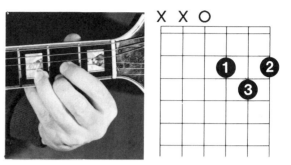

Bm

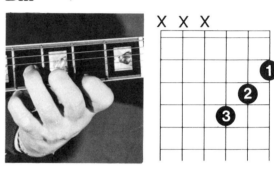

You can play exactly the same strum that's used on the recording by playing only downstrokes (one on each beat). Sometimes, as indicated in the notation below, you'll strum a chord and let it ring for two full measures. In the chorus section, use the basic strum (down-up on each beat).

Roxanne
Words and Music by The Police

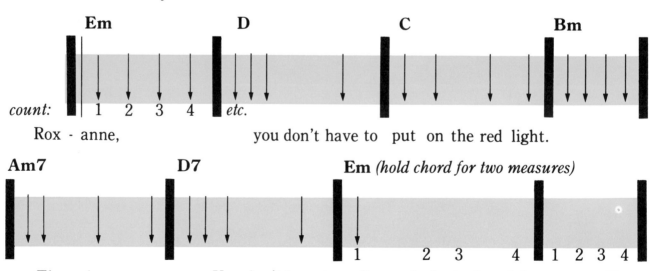

Em   **D**   **C**   **Bm**

count: 1   2   3   4   *etc.*

Rox - anne,   you don't have to put on the red light.

Am7   **D7**   **Em** *(hold chord for two measures)*

1   2   3   4   1   2   3   4

Those days are o - ver. You don't have to sell your body to the night.   Rox -

Roxanne *continued*

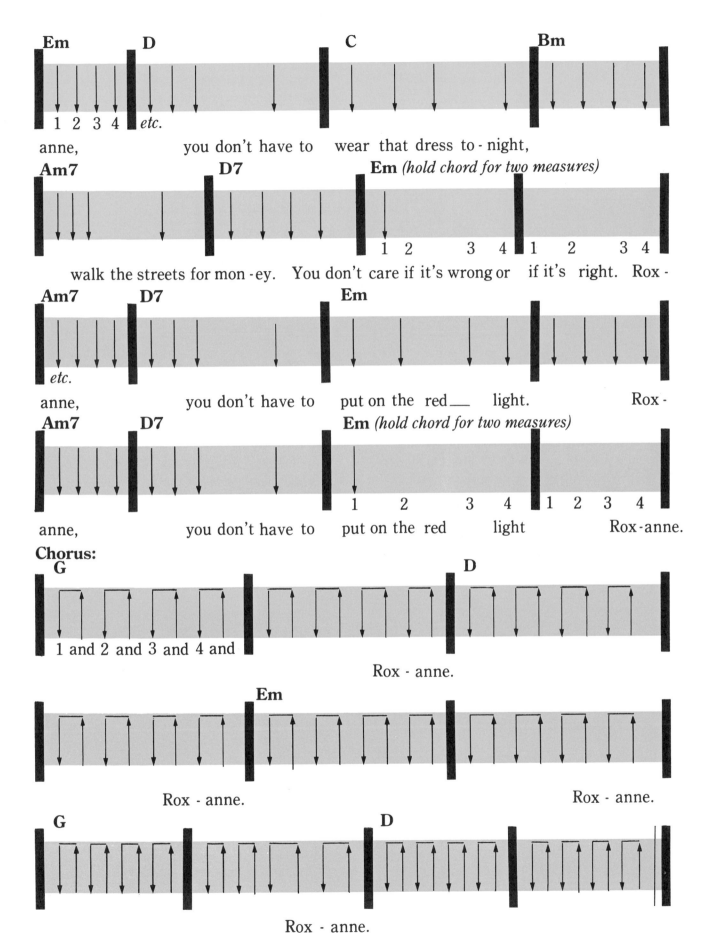

anne, you don't have to wear that dress to - night,

walk the streets for mon - ey. You don't care if it's wrong or if it's right. Rox -

anne, you don't have to put on the red ___ light. Rox -

anne, you don't have to put on the red light Rox - anne.

Chorus:

Rox - anne.

Rox - anne. Rox - anne.

Rox - anne.

Great Balls of Fire

One of the original wild men of rock is rockabilly master Jerry Lee Lewis. Many of his recordings have become rock 'n' roll classics. I'd like to teach you one of them, the irresistible "Great Balls of Fire."

First we need to learn a new chord, **E7**

E7

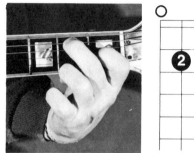 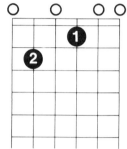

You can play this song with a down-up, down-up, down-up, down-up pattern; but once you get the chords going, I'd like you to try a strumming variation to make the song rock a little bit more. In this variation you will make a percussive sound. Place your right-hand palm against the strings, near the bridge. With your wrist only, brush the strings as if you were playing a regular chord. This should produce a sound that sounds like "chick." Now, finger any chord. Play the down-up, down-up, down-up, down-up rhythm, except on the second and fourth "down," press your palm against the strings and play the "chick" sound. This will give you a rhythm that sounds as if a drummer is playing along on the second and fourth beat.

The exercise below will help you get into it. It takes a little bit of practice, but this technique can really juice up your playing.

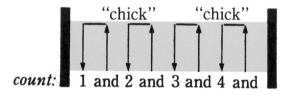

Let's try out this new technique on "Great Balls of Fire." As indicated in the notation below, strum the last chord once and let it ring for two measures.

Great Balls of Fire

Words and Music by Otis Blackwell and Jack Hammer

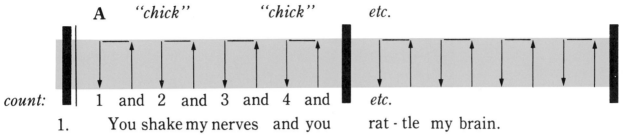

A   *"chick"*   *"chick"*   *etc.*

count: 1 and 2 and 3 and 4 and   *etc.*

1.   You shake my nerves and you   rat-tle my brain.
2.   I laughed at love __ 'cause I   thought it was fun-ny.

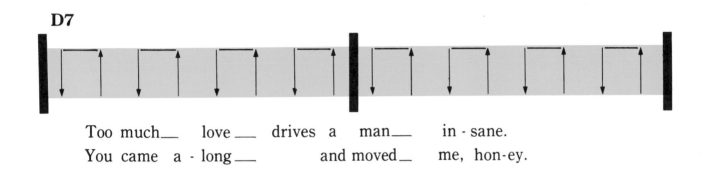

D7

Too much __ love __ drives a man __ in-sane.
You came a-long __ and moved __ me, hon-ey.

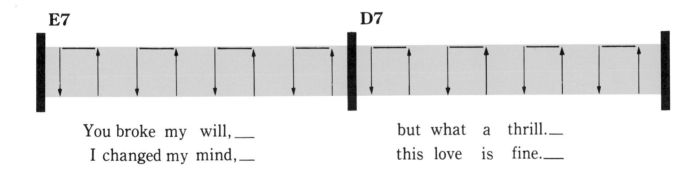

E7   **D7**

You broke my will, __   but what a thrill. __
I changed my mind, __   this love is fine. __

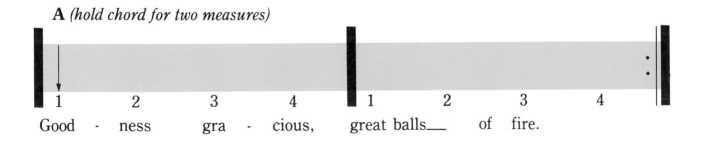

A *(hold chord for two measures)*

1   2   3   4   1   2   3   4

Good - ness gra - cious, great balls __ of fire.

Black Magic Woman

Carlos Santana brought a Latin influence into rock 'n' roll with great success. One of his most famous songs is "Black Magic Woman." We can play this song with our basic strum (down-up, down-up, down-up, down-up). First, let's learn one more new chord, **B7**.

B7

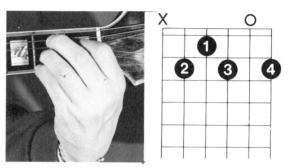

Black Magic Woman
By Peter Green

Em

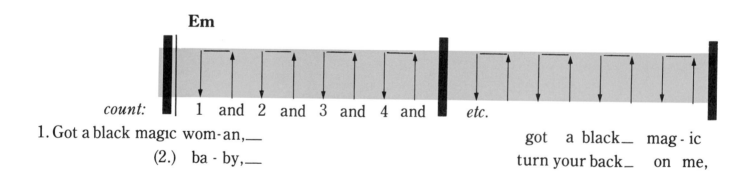

count: 1 and 2 and 3 and 4 and   *etc.*

1. Got a black magic wom-an,___   got a black___ mag-ic
   (2.) ba - by,___   turn your back___ on me,

B7

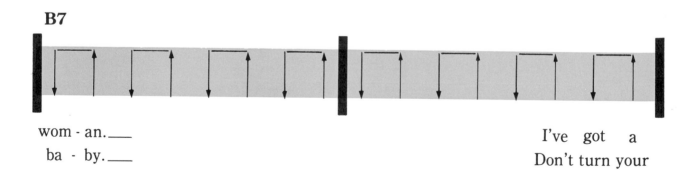

wom - an.___   I've got a
ba - by.___   Don't turn your

Black Magic Woman *continued*

Em

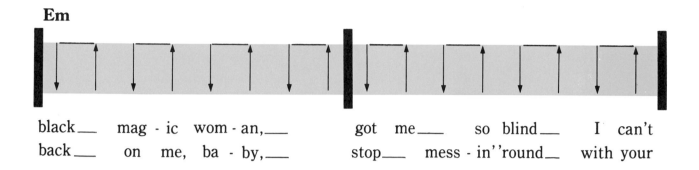

black__ mag - ic wom - an,__   got me__ so blind__ I can't
back__ on me, ba - by,__   stop__ mess - in''round__ with your

Am7

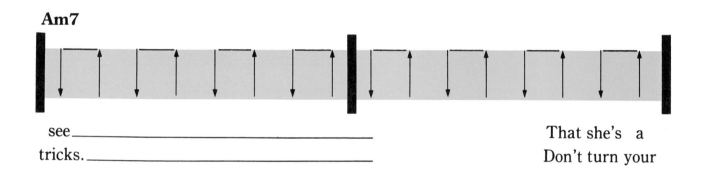

see_____   That she's a
tricks._____   Don't turn your

Em   **B7**

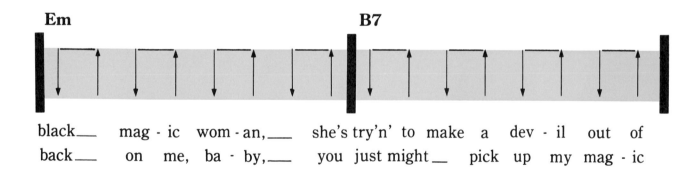

black__ mag - ic wom - an,__ she's try'n' to make a dev - il out of
back__ on me, ba - by,__ you just might__ pick up my mag - ic

Em

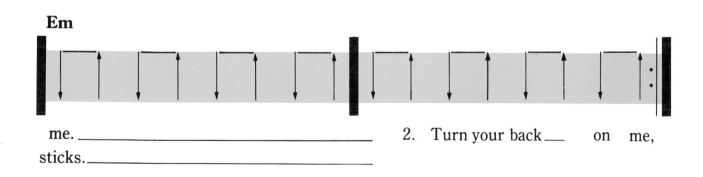

me._____   2. Turn your back__ on me,
sticks._____

21

Riffs

Johnny B. Goode

Chuck Berry is one of rock music's most influential guitarists and songwriters. His songs have become rock standards, and every rock guitarist should know them.

The one song that probably best captures the spirit of rock 'n' roll is "Johnny B. Goode." Because this song is so important, I want to show you two ways to play it. First, let's learn a new chord, **E.**

E

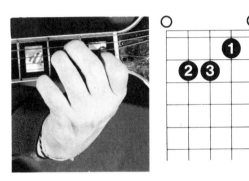

In this version of "Johnny B. Goode," use the down, down, down-up, down-up strumming pattern (Strumming Pattern 2).

Johnny B. Goode
Words and Music by Chuck Berry

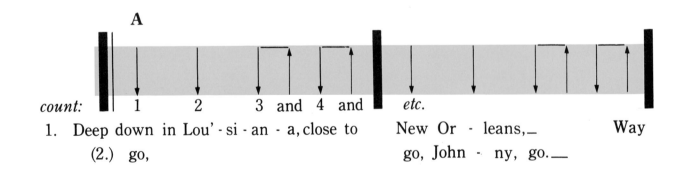

count: 1   2   3 and 4 and   etc.

1. Deep down in Lou' - si - an - a, close to   New Or - leans,___   Way
(2.) go,   go, John - ny, go.___

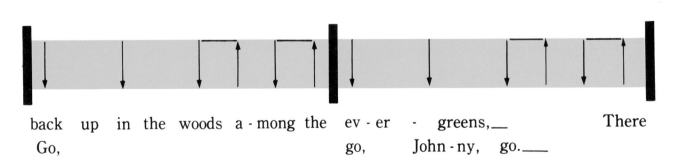

back up in the woods a - mong the ev - er - greens,___   There
Go,   go,   John - ny, go.___

Johnny B. Goode *continued*

D

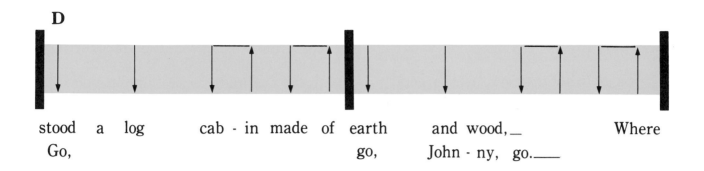

stood   a   log   cab - in made of   earth   and wood, __   Where
Go,   go,   John - ny, go. __

A

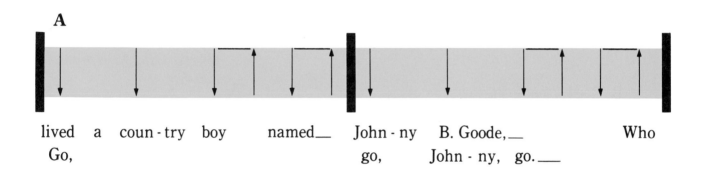

lived   a   coun - try boy   named __   John - ny   B. Goode, __   Who
Go,   go,   John - ny, go. __

E

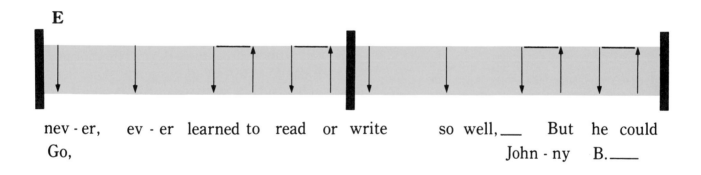

nev - er,   ev - er learned to read or write   so well, __   But he could
Go,   John - ny   B. __

A

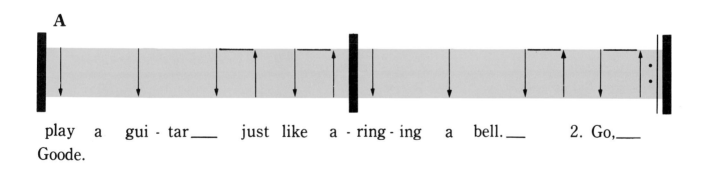

play   a   gui - tar __   just like a - ring - ing a bell. __   2. Go, __
Goode.

In the next version of "Johnny B. Goode," instead of playing chords, we are going to play **riffs**.

A riff is a melodic fragment, usually very rhythmic, that can form the basic accompaniment for a song. The riff to use for "Johnny B. Goode" was made famous by Chuck Berry himself. In fact, it's often called the **Chuck Berry riff.**

You can play the riff instead of playing chords. Or, if a second guitarist is playing chords, you can play the riff as a lead guitar part.

"Johnny B. Goode" uses three chords: **A, D,** and **E.** The Chuck Berry riff can be substituted for each of these chords, as long as the riff is played on the proper strings. For example, to play the riff that goes with the **A** chord, place your first finger at the second fret of the fourth string. Now play two downstrokes, hitting only the fifth string (open) and the fourth string (fretted as indicated). Next add your third finger at the fourth fret of the fourth string (still holding down your first finger on the second fret) and play two more downstrokes. These four downstrokes are played in the same rhythm that you used for two down-up strums in the basic strum:

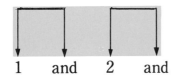

The diagram below shows the Chuck Berry riff (in **A**) as it is played on the neck.

Play these two strings only.

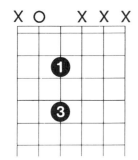

This finger stays down throughout.

This finger plays two off and two on.

Another way to show the same riff is to use a form of guitar notation called **tablature.** The six-line tablature staff graphically represents the six strings of the guitar, with the top line representing the high **E** string. Numbers designate the frets to be played, and a zero indicates an open string. As in standard notation, bar lines are used to group the beats into measures.

Here is how the Chuck Berry riff (in **A**) looks in tablature.

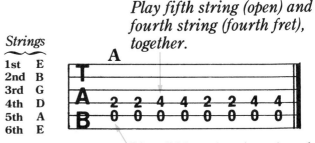

Play fifth string (open) and fourth string (fourth fret), together.

Play fifth string (open) and fourth string (second fret), together.

You can play the Chuck Berry riff that goes with the **D** chord by playing the same finger pattern that went with the **A** chord, except on strings four and three.

In diagram form the riff in **D** looks like this:

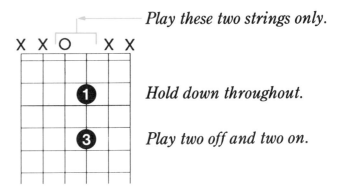

Play these two strings only.

Hold down throughout.

Play two off and two on.

In tablature it looks like this:

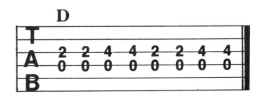

Again, the same finger pattern is used to play the Chuck Berry riff on an **E** chord, except now you'll use strings six and five.

Here is how the **E** riff looks in diagram form and in tablature:

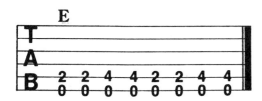

Play these two strings only.

Hold down throughout.

Play two off and two on.

Now we're ready to play "Johnny B. Goode" using riffs instead of chords. When you get it down, I'm sure you'll hear how these riffs can really make the difference between just strumming along and really rocking. Remember to play downstrokes throughout, and play as rhythmically as possible. Also, try to associate each riff with its proper chord symbol (placed above the tablature staff) so that as you progress you'll be able to substitute these riffs for the normal chords.

Johnny B. Goode

Riffs

1. Deep down in Lou'-si - an - a, close to   New Or - leans,_   Way
(2.) go,   go,   John-ny, go._

back up in the woods a-mong the   ev - er - greens,_   There
Go,   go,   John-ny, go._

stood a log__ cab - in made of earth__ and wood,_   Where
Go,   go,   John-ny, go.__

lived a coun-try boy __ named__   John - ny B. Goode,_   Who
Go,   go,   John-ny, go.__

nev - er, ev - er learned to read or write __ so well,_ But he could
Go,   John-ny B. __

play a gui-tar__ just like a - ring-ing a bell.__ 2. Go,__
Goode. _

Sus4 to the Floor

Sometimes it's possible to play a chord and a riff at the same time. One way to do this is to alternately add and remove a finger on one string while strumming a chord. For example, with a **D** chord, you can add your fourth finger to the third fret of the first string. This changes the chord from **D** to **D Suspended Fourth (Dsus4).**

D

 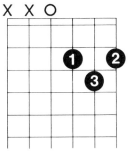

Dsus4

 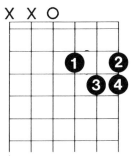

With a **C** chord, you can add your fourth finger to the third fret of the fourth string, producing a **Csus4** chord. (When strumming **Csus4,** tilt your first finger so that it gently presses against the first string, blocking out the sound.)

C

 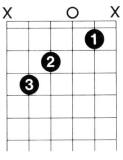

Csus4

 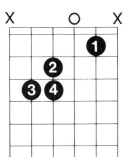

"Sus4 to the Floor" is a piece I've written to get you used to playing **sus4** chords. You'll also play two new strumming patterns. The first pattern (in the first eight measures) is a down, down-up, down, down strum. The second pattern (in the last eight measures) is a "start-stop" rhythm that can be very exciting, especially when playing with a drummer.

To play this start-stop pattern, play a downstroke on beat one, then rest (don't play) on beats two and three, then play a downstroke on beat four. The important thing to remember is that while resting, don't let the sound (from beat one) carry over into the empty beats. This can be accomplished by covering the strings with your right hand until it's time to strum again. This way, your left-hand fingers can remain in place. When done correctly, this effect produces a very rhythmic feel.

Riffs

Sus4 to the Floor
Music by Steve Tarshis

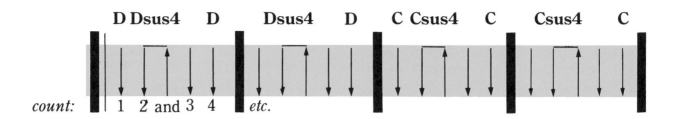

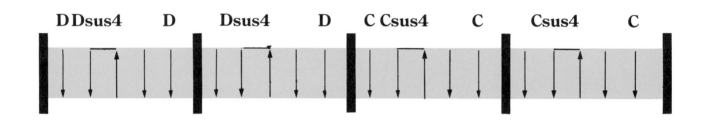

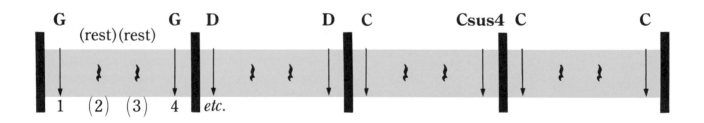

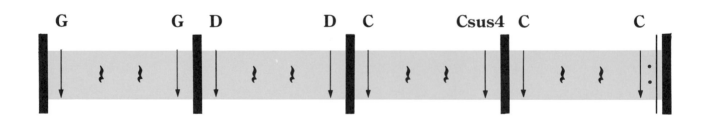

Closing Comments

That's it for now. **Book 1** has given you what I hope will be a good foundation for rock 'n' roll guitar playing. The best, however, is yet to come. Practice what you've learned in **Book 1,** and I'll see you in **Book 2.** Remember, the more you practice, the more you'll rock!

The Complete Rock Guitar Player.

by Steve Tarshis.

Book Two.

Amsco Publications
New York/London/Sydney/Cologne

Contents

The Songs

About This Book

Welcome to **Book 2**. You're no longer a guitar rookie. You know some chords, you can play a few songs, and you can even play a riff or two.

You will be learning a lot more about strumming, a whole handful of new chords and riffs, and some more of the greatest rock songs of all time — so let's get right into it.

Stand by Me

Let's start right off with a new chord, the **F** chord. This chord introduces an important concept in rock guitar—**barring** (holding down more than one string with one finger). Barring takes a bit of practice, but it won't be too difficult once you get the hang of it.

F

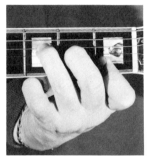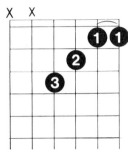

Notice that the first finger holds down both the first and second strings. Your first finger should lie flat across the strings. To produce the pressure needed to hold down both strings, bend in on the joint and squeeze, with the thumb in position in the middle of the back of the neck. The second and third fingers play as usual, with the tips. Remember, the best sound is produced by pressing each finger as close to the metal fret bar as possible without actually touching it.

Here's another new chord that's somewhat easier to play—**Am.** The fingering for the **Am** chord is the same as the fingering for **Am7** (which you learned in **Book 1**), except that your third finger is added is added at the second fret of the third string.

Am

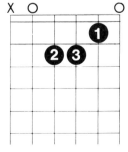

Now let's put these two new chords together with some more familiar onces to play one of rock's most tried and true chord progressions. "Stand by Me," is a rock classic. Originally recorded by Ben E. King, it was later covered by John Lennon.

To play this song, use Strumming Pattern 2 (down, down, down-up, down-up). Remember, when changing chords, move only those fingers that will be on a new string or fret. For example, when changing from **C** to **Am**, your first and second fingers stay in place.

Some New Chords

Stand by Me
Words and Music by Ben E. King, Jerry Lieber and Mike Stoller

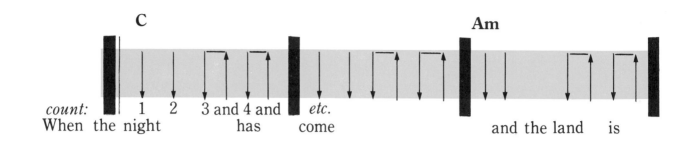

count: 1 2 3 and 4 and *etc.*

When the night has come   and the land is

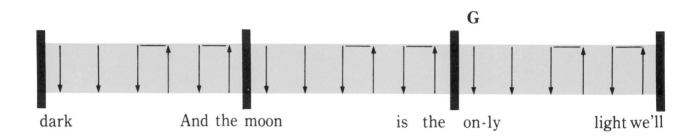

dark   And the moon   is the on-ly   light we'll

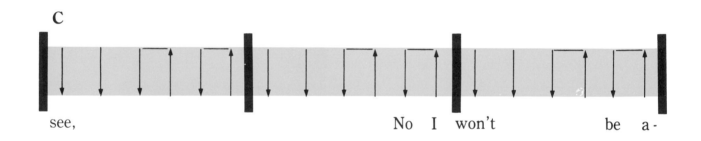

see,   No I won't   be a-

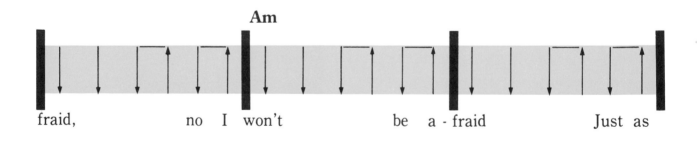

fraid,   no I won't   be a-fraid   Just as

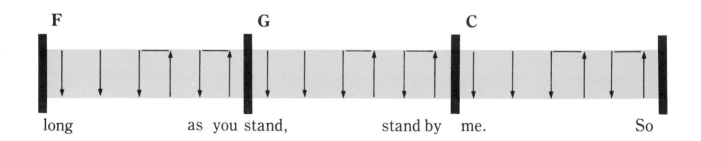

long   as you stand,   stand by me.   So

Copyright © by Progressive Music Publishing Co., Inc., Trio Music, Inc.,
and ADT Enterprises, Inc.
All rights for the U.S.A. and Canada controlled by Unichappell Music, Inc.
(Rightsong Music, Publisher)
This Arrangement Copyright © 1987 by Unichappell Music, Inc., Trio Music Inc.
and ADT Enterprises, Inc.
International Copyright Secured. All Rights Reserved. Used by Permission.

6

Stand by Me *continued*

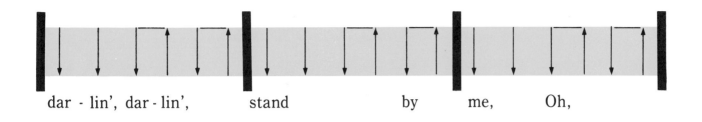

dar - lin', dar - lin',   stand   by   me,   Oh,

Am   **F**

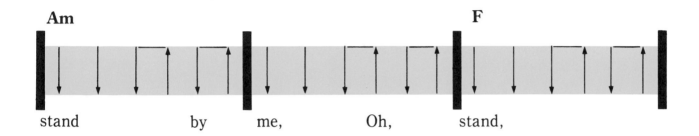

stand   by   me,   Oh,   stand,

G   **C**

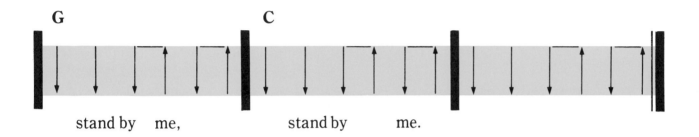

stand by   me,   stand by   me.

Every Breath You Take

Many chord progressions (such as the one we used for "Stand by Me") are used for more than one song. Most of "Every Breath You Take," by the Police, uses the same chord progression as "Stand by Me."

I want to show you one more new chord before we start. The **G7** chord is a variation of the **G** chord. It occurs at the end of the **bridge** of "Every Breath You Take." (The bridge of a song is a middle section that usually occurs between the second verse and the third verse.) In "Every Breath You Take," the **G7** chord helps lead from the bridge back into the verse.

G7

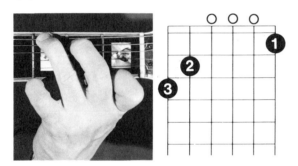

To play "Every Breath You Take," use the same strum you used for "Stand by Me"— down, down, down-up, down-up.

Every Breath You Take
Words and Music By The Police

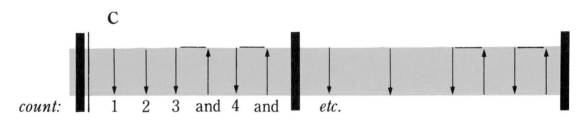

C

count: 1 2 3 and 4 and   *etc.*

1. Ev -'ry breath you take,   ev - 'ry move   you

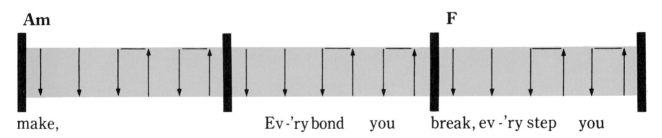

Am   F

make,   Ev -'ry bond you   break, ev -'ry step you

Every Breath You Take *continued*

G   **Am**

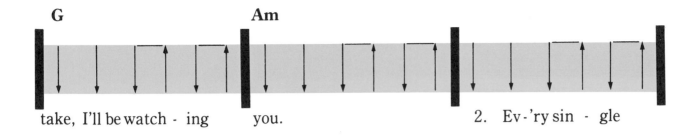

take, I'll be watch - ing   you.   2. Ev - 'ry sin - gle

C   **Am**

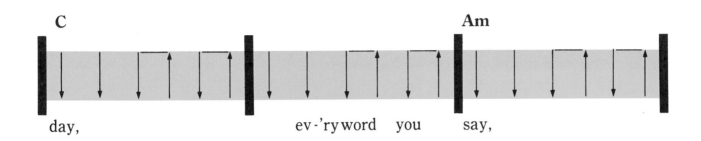

day,   ev - 'ry word   you   say,

                   F   **G**

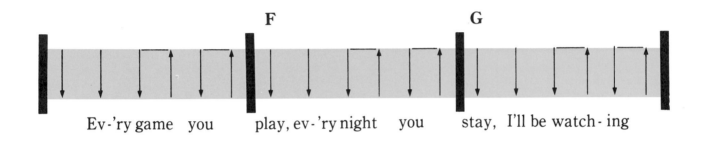

Ev - 'ry game   you   play, ev - 'ry night   you   stay, I'll be watch - ing

C   **Bridge:**   **F**

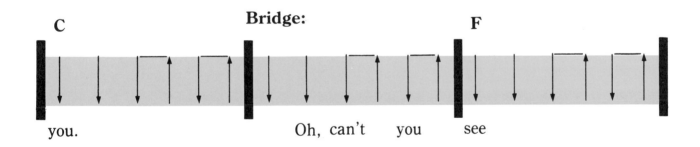

you.   Oh, can't   you   see

                   C

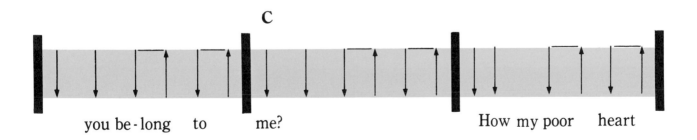

you be - long   to   me?   How my poor   heart

Every Breath You Take *continued*

D

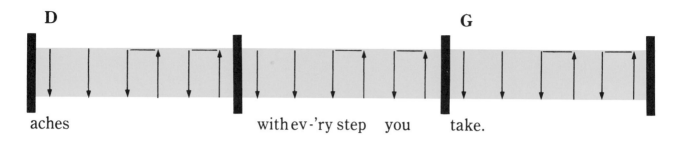

aches   with ev-'ry step   you   take.

G7   **C**

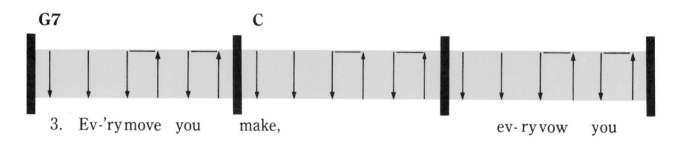

3.   Ev-'ry move   you   make,   ev-ry vow   you

Am   **F**

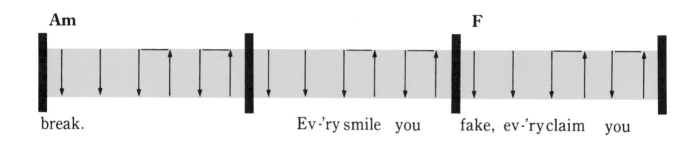

break.   Ev-'ry smile   you   fake, ev-'ry claim   you

G   **Am**

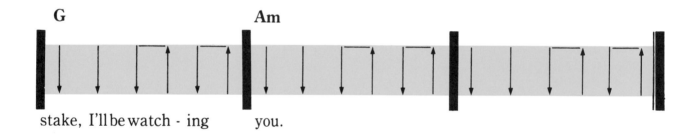

stake, I'll be watch - ing   you.

I Saw Her Standing There

Finger an **E** chord and add your fourth finger to the third fret of the second string. This produces an **E7** chord.

E7

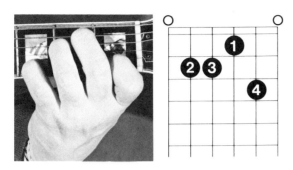

This **E7** chord is a fuller version of the **E7** chord you learned in **Book 1.** You will find that the more you play, the more you'll discover alternate versions of chords.

Seventh chords have a bluesy, funky kind of sound. Songs that use **E7** often use **B7** and **A7** as well. Chords that are often found together are referred to by musicians as being in the same **key**. We'll learn more about keys as we go along.

Now let's use these chords to play the Beatles' "I Saw Her Standing There." Use the down, down, down-up, down-up pattern. You'll notice that the form of the song is verse, verse, bridge, verse—the same format we saw in "Every Breath You Take."

I Saw Her Standing There
Words and Music by John Lennon and Paul McCartney

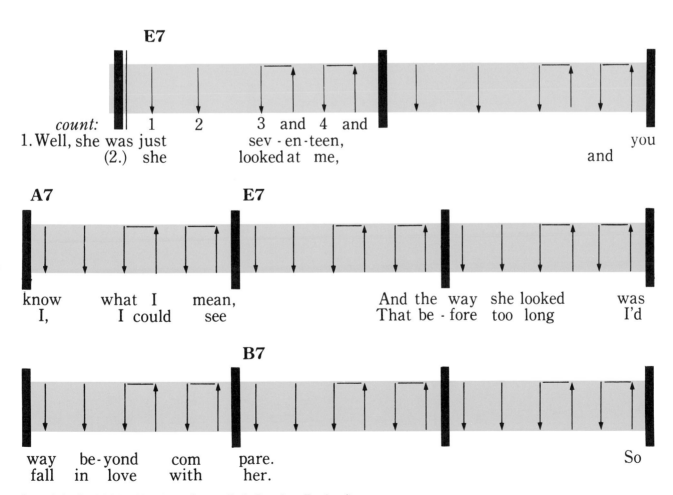

E7

count: 1 2 3 and 4 and

1. Well, she was just sev-en-teen, you
(2.) she looked at me, and

A7   **E7**

know what I mean, And the way she looked was
I, I could see That be-fore too long I'd

B7

way be-yond com pare. So
fall in love with her.

Some New Chords

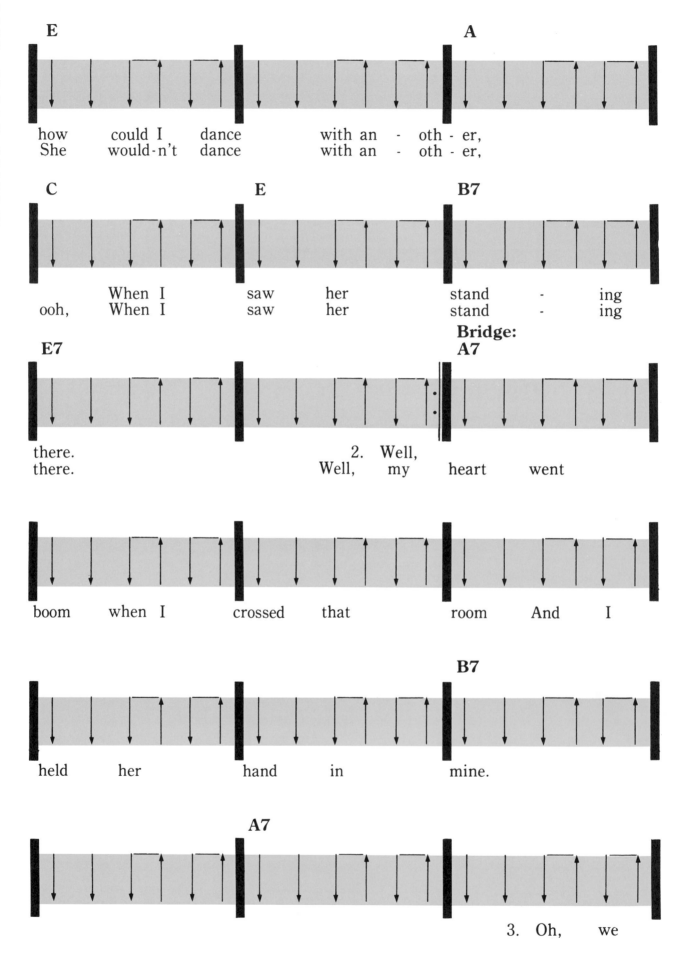

E   **A**

how   could I   dance   with an - oth-er,
She   would-n't dance   with an - oth-er,

C   **E**   **B7**

ooh,   When I   saw   her   stand -   ing
        When I   saw   her   stand -   ing

E7   **Bridge:**
                                      A7

there.   2. Well,
there.   Well, my   heart   went

boom   when I   crossed   that   room   And   I

                                      B7

held   her   hand   in   mine.

           A7

                                  3. Oh, we

I Saw Her Standing There *continued*

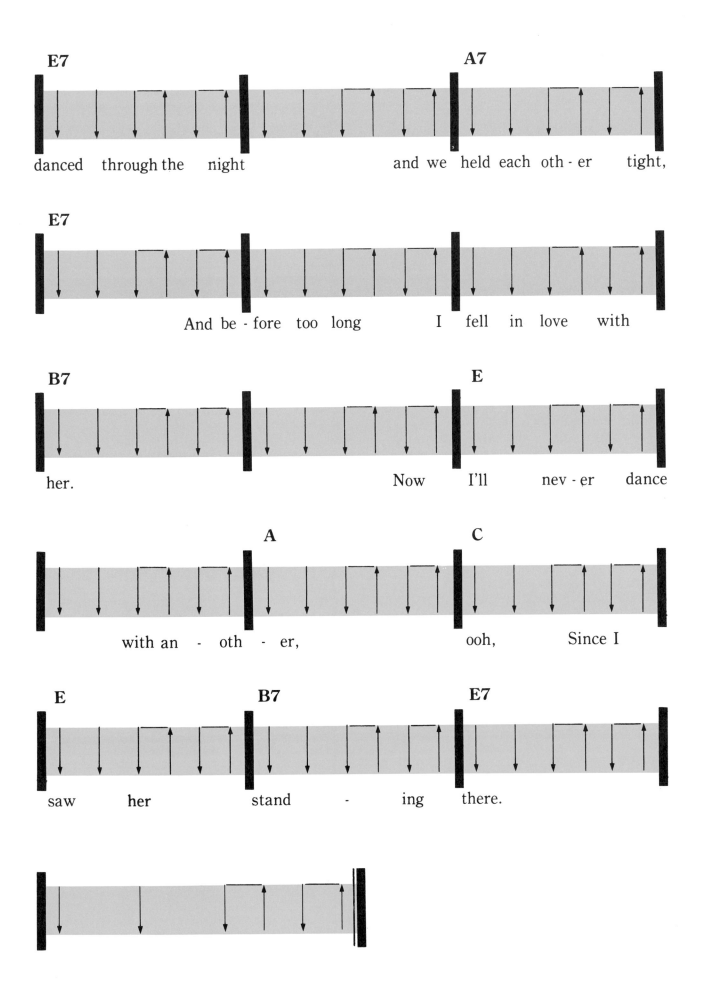

E7
danced   through the   night   **A7** and we   held each oth - er   tight,

E7
                    And be - fore   too   long   I   fell   in   love   with

B7
her.   **E** Now   I'll   nev - er   dance

                    A with an   -   oth   -   er,   **C** ooh,   Since I

E
saw   her   **B7** stand   -   ing   **E7** there.

13

Sunshine of Your Love

The more you get into playing rock guitar, the more you can see that just strumming chords isn't always enough.

"Sunshine of Your Love" was a massive hit for Cream in the late sixties. This song secured Eric Clapton's reputation as one of the world's greatest rock guitarists, and it established Cream as the inventors of the power trio sound that still serves as a basis for today's metal bands.

For this song we're going to combine a riff with chord accompaniment to make the song sound "real." First, here's the basic riff that Eric Clapton played. I've notated it (in tablature) so that you can play all the notes on the sixth string (the low **E** string).

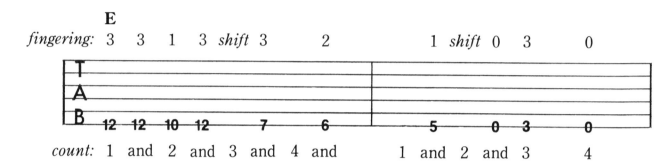

As you can see, this riff covers almost the entire range of the neck. The first four notes are all played in the same position; that is, your left hand stays in one place (with your first finger at the tenth fret). To play the next three notes you must shift to a new position (with your first finger at the fifth fret). Finally, one more shift is made to play the last three notes.

The idea in **position playing** is to play as many notes in one position as you can before shifting. This makes your playing faster and smoother. It's important to use the correct fingering within each position for the sake of speed and clarity. Although we aren't concerned with speed at this stage, later on you'll want to have established good fingering habits so you'll be able to play those lightning-fast leads.

In "Sunshine of Your Love," the basic riff is played four times on the sixth string. Then it is played two times on the fifth string (the **A** string). Here is the notation for the riff on the **A** string. Notice that the fingerings and the positions are exactly as they were on the low **E** string.

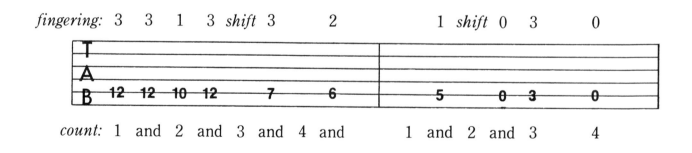

"Sunshine of Your Love" is a song that uses both riffs and chords. The chord section of the song uses **B7, D** and **A.** On the recording you can hear that the first of these chords has a strumming rhythm that is staggered a bit. It might be described as "long, short, long." It's the same as the normal down-up, down strum, except that the first "down" is held a bit longer than usual and the "up" a bit shorter than usual. As you can see in the notation below this is followed by two beats of rest, and then the **D** and **A** chords are held for two beats each. After this pattern is played three times, the **B7** chord is strummed eight times (one beat each). For simplicity's sake, I have put this song in a different key from the original recording; however, you should listen to the record to help you get the feel.

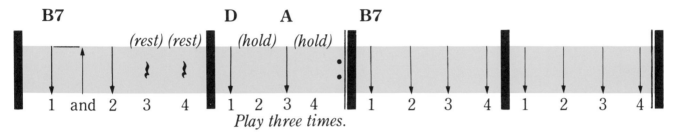

Play three times.

Once you've practiced the riffs and chords separately, you'll be able to put it all together.

Sunshine of Your Love
Words and Music by Jack Bruce, Peter Brown and Eric Clapton

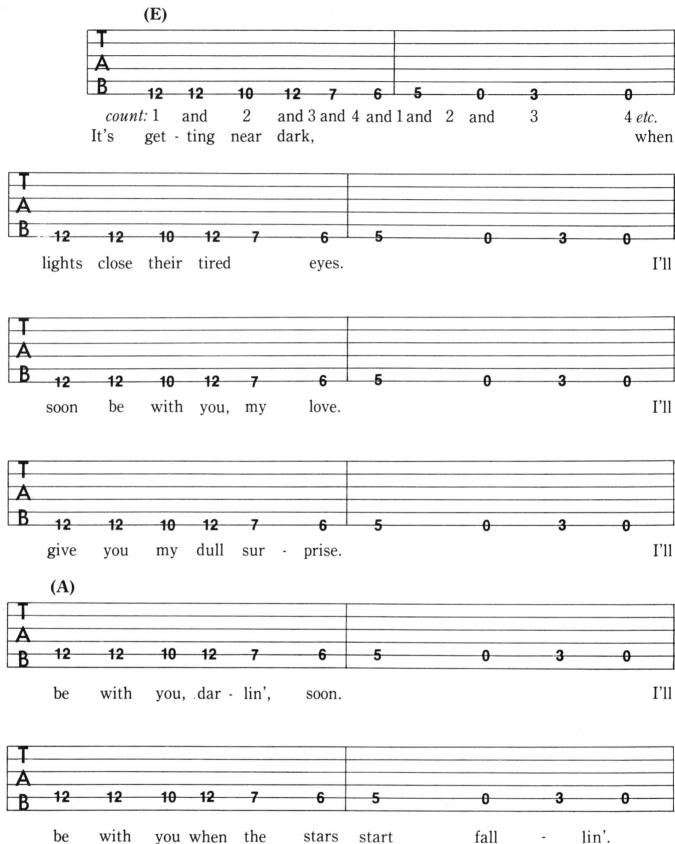

(E)

count: 1 and 2 and 3 and 4 and 1 and 2 and 3 4 *etc.*

It's get - ting near dark, when

lights close their tired eyes. I'll

soon be with you, my love. I'll

give you my dull sur - prise. I'll

(A)

be with you, dar - lin', soon. I'll

be with you when the stars start fall - lin'.

Sunshine of Your Love *continued*

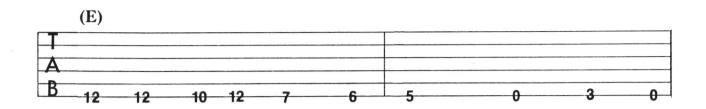

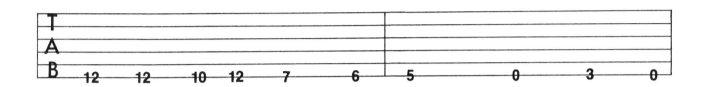

B7   **D**   **A**

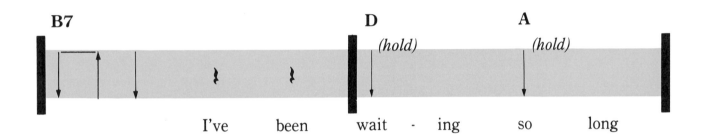

I've   been   wait - ing   so   long

B7   **D**   **A**

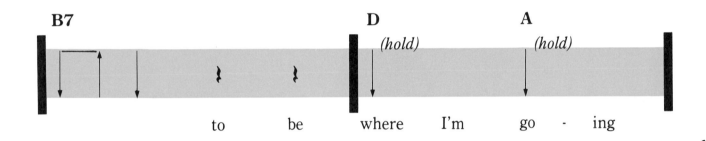

to   be   where   I'm   go - ing

B7   **D**   **A**

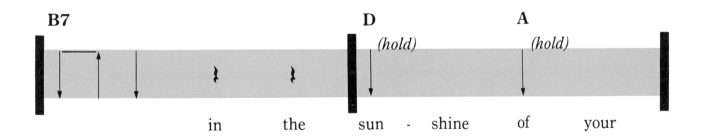

in   the   sun - shine   of   your

B7

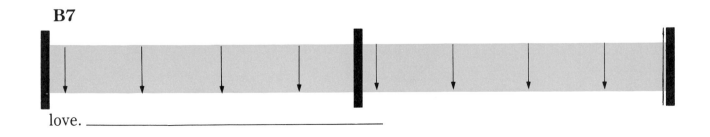

love. _____

Hey Joe

"Hey Joe," made famous by Jimi Hendrix, is another song that uses both chords and riffs. Like a lot of rock songs, "Hey Joe" is in the key of **E**. This means that **E** is the main chord of the song and the one that all the other chords seem to lead to.

"We'll start with the basic strum of down-up, down-up, down-up, down-up, but with a variation. Beats one and three will be **accented.** When a note or chord is accented, it is played with a strong emphasis. Also, for all the other beats ("and-two-and" and "and-four-and"), we'll play more softly and we'll hit only the lower strings of the chord. The overall effect of this strum will be very dramatic when you master it.

Let's try out this strum on one chord, an **E** chord.

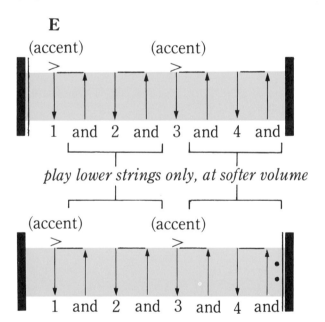

Like "Sunshine of Your Love," "Hey Joe" uses a riff in combination with chords. The riff to "Hey Joe" is a simple one, as you can see in the notation below. Begin the riff on the "and" of beat three. Listening to the record will help you get the exact rhythmic feel.

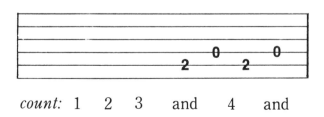

For measures one and two of "Hey Joe," use the strumming variation with accents on beats one and three and soft, low-string strumming on the other beats. Play measures three and four as indicated: three strums on the **E** chord and then the riff.

Again, notice how the use of chords in combination with riffs really helps to make the song come alive.

Hey Joe

Words and Music by William M. Roberts

Riffs

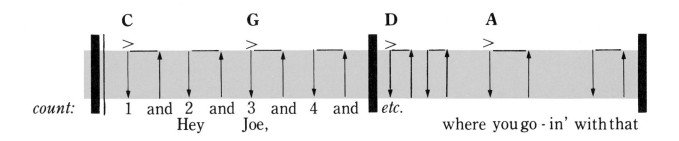

count: 1 and 2 and 3 and 4 and *etc.*
Hey Joe, where you go - in' with that

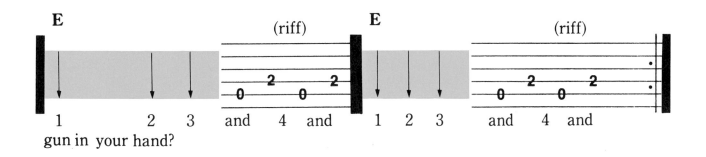

1 2 3 and 4 and 1 2 3 and 4 and
gun in your hand?

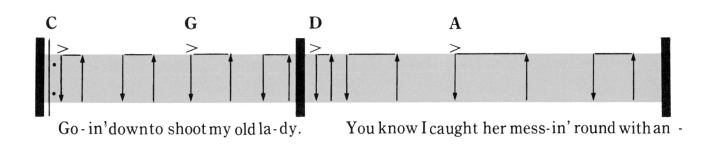

Go - in' down to shoot my old la - dy. You know I caught her mess-in' round with an -

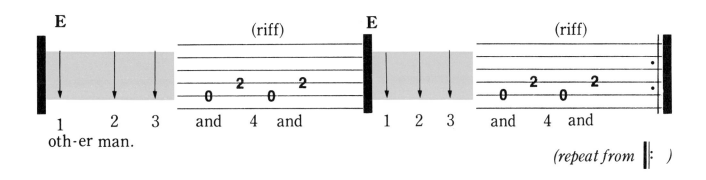

1 2 3 and 4 and 1 2 3 and 4 and
oth-er man.

(repeat from 𝄆 *)*

Space Oddity

To play David Bowie's "Space Oddity," we need to learn one more new chord, **Fm.** In this chord your first finger will be playing three strings at once, so it may take a bit of work.

Use the same strumming pattern that you used at the beginning of "Hey Joe": accents on beats one and three and soft, low-string strumming on the other beats.

Fm

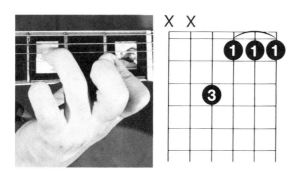

Space Oddity
Words and Music by David Bowie

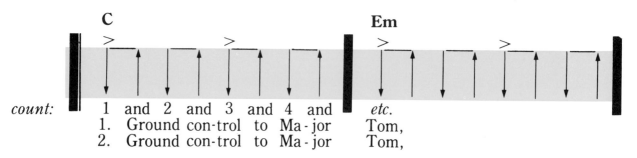

count: 1   and   2   and   3   and   4   and   *etc.*
1. Ground con-trol to Ma-jor   Tom,
2. Ground con-trol to Ma-jor   Tom,

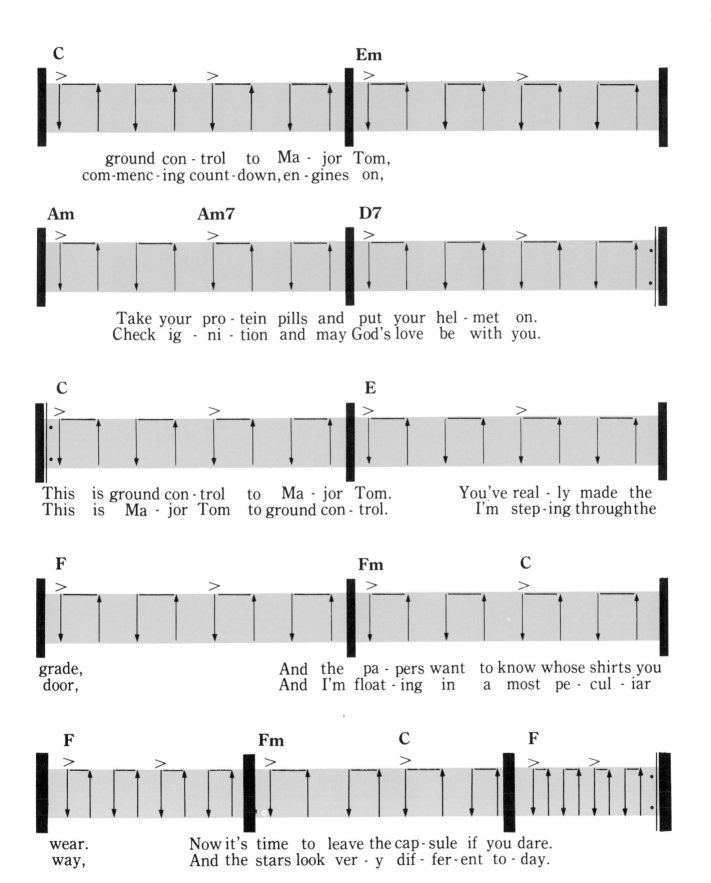

C

Em

ground con-trol to Ma-jor Tom,
com-menc-ing count-down, en-gines on,

Am **Am7** **D7**

Take your pro-tein pills and put your hel-met on.
Check ig-ni-tion and may God's love be with you.

C **E**

This is ground con-trol to Ma-jor Tom.
This is Ma-jor Tom to ground con-trol.

You've real-ly made the
I'm step-ing through the

F **Fm** **C**

grade,
door,

And the pa-pers want to know whose shirts you
And I'm float-ing in a most pe-cul-iar

F **Fm** **C** **F**

wear.
way,

Now it's time to leave the cap-sule if you dare.
And the stars look ver-y dif-fer-ent to-day.

More About Riffs

You've seen how riffs combined with chords can really make a song come alive. Sometimes the lead guitarist in a band will play a riff while the rhythm guitarist in a band will play a riff while the rhythm guitarist or keyboard player supplies the chords. These riffs are very important to a song and are identified as the song's "signature."

I want to show you some of these signature riffs so that you can have some fun with them while practicing your single-note playing. But first let's talk a little about music notation and theory. All the riffs I'm about to show you will be written in both tablature and standard music notation. You already know about tablature, so let's talk about standard notation.

The chart below shows how the notes on the first three frets look in both standard notation and tablature. The chart also names the notes.

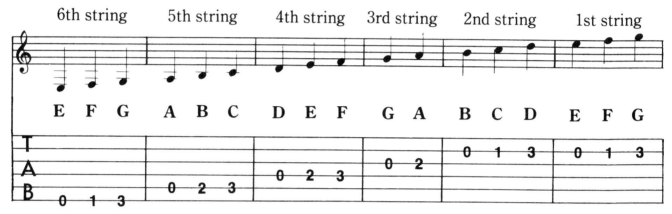

The next chart gives the **time values** for different kinds of notes. The time value of a note indicates how long it will be held.

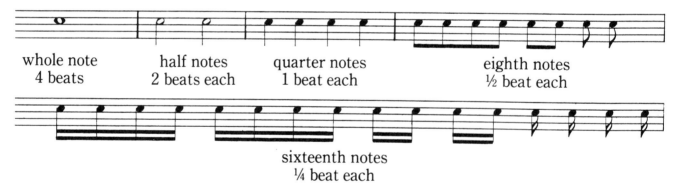

whole note
4 beats

half notes
2 beats each

quarter notes
1 beat each

eighth notes
½ beat each

sixteenth notes
¼ beat each

A **sharp** (#) in front of a note will raise that note one fret. (The musical distance from one fret to the next is called a **half step**.) A **flat** (♭) in front of a note will lower that note one fret (one half-step). When a sharp or flat appears in front of a note, it also affects all other notes of the same pitch that follow it until it is cancelled by the end of the measure or by a **natural** sign (♮).

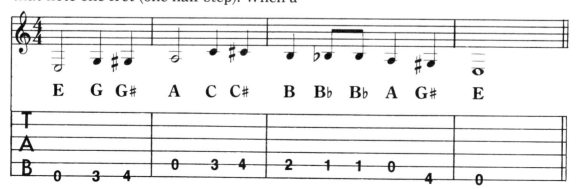

A **key signature** is a group of sharps or flats that appear at the beginning of a piece of music. The key signature shows that certain notes will be sharped or flatted throughout the entire song.

A **time signature** is a set of two numbers, one above the other, that appears at the beginning of a piece of music (right after the key signature). The top number tells how many beats will be in each measure, and the bottom number tells what kind of note will receive one beat. Most rock songs are written in $\frac{4}{4}$ time, which means that each measure contains four beats and a quarter note receives one beat.

key signature: all **F**s, **C**s, and **G**s are sharped throughout.

time signature: four beats per measure; quarter note receives one beat.

key signature: all **B**s, **E**s, and **A**s are flatted throughout.

Notice that there is a dot after the last half-note above. When a dot is placed after a note, it increases the time value of that note by one-half. Don't worry too much about the music notation for now. As long as you can work out the tablature and you are familiar with the riff, you won't have much of a problem.

More About Riffs

The first signature riff I want to show you goes with the first song you learned in **Book 1,** the Rolling Stones "Miss You." I've written the chords above the riff so a second guitarist can strum along. (Or, if you have a tape recorder, you can record the chords first and then play the riff along with the tape.) The curved line in measure three is called a **tie.** When two notes are "tied" together, only the first note is played and the pitch is sustained for the combined time value of both notes.

The Beatles' George Harrison played this riff, which was the signature of "Day Tripper."

Here's Deep Purple's famous riff to "Smoke on the Water." The whole band played it along with lead guitarist Ritchie Blackmore, so there are no accompanying chords.

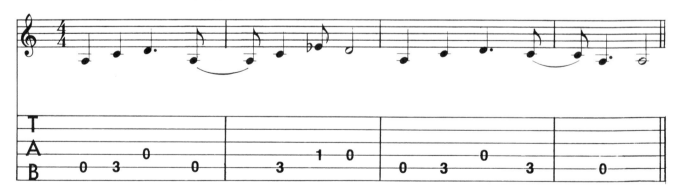

24

Here's an all-purpose rock 'n' roll riff that you can try out. I call it "Real Rock 'n' Roll."

Eddie Van Halen plays a riff similar to this on Michael Jackson's "Beat It."

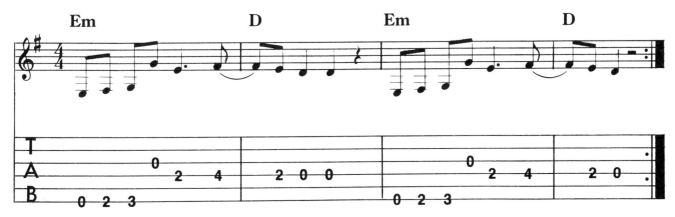

Remember: all Fs are sharped throughout.

The Shuffle

The **shuffle** is one of rock 'n' roll's most useful and effective rhythms. This rhythm was used in rock's early days in songs such as Elvis Presley's "Don't Be Cruel," Buddy Holly's "That'll Be the Day," the Everly Brothers' "('Til) I Kissed You," and Chuck Berry's "No Particular Place to Go." The Beach Boys used it in "Help Me, Rhonda" and "California Girls." The Beatles used it in "Penny Lane" and "With a Little Help From My Friends." The Rolling Stones used it in "Have You Seen Your Mother, Baby, Standing in the Shadow." And that's just skimming the surface.

To understand the basic shuffle rhythm, let's compare it to the basic strum of down-up, down-up, down-up, down-up. The way to play a shuffle is to hold each "down" a little bit longer than usual, and then make each "up" a little bit shorter. Each down-up of the shuffle rhythm takes up the same amount of time as one down-up of the basic strum, but in the shuffle the "down" and the "up" are not of equal value.

To practice the shuffle rhythm, think down-rest-up, down-rest-up, down-rest-up, down-rest-up for each measure. Each beat is like a fast "one-two-three" with the "down" coming on "one" and the "up" coming on "three." Try this out on one chord, as in the notation below. Practice slowly at first, and then gradually pick up the tempo until you get the feel of it.

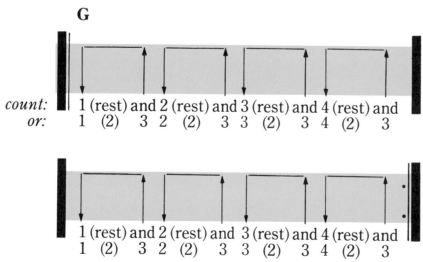

G

count: 1 (rest) and 2 (rest) and 3 (rest) and 4 (rest) and
or: 1 (2)   3 2 (2)   3 3 (2)   3 4 (2)   3

1 (rest) and 2 (rest) and 3 (rest) and 4 (rest) and
1 (2)   3 2 (2)   3 3 (2)   3 4 (2)   3

Revolution

The Beatles' "Revolution" is a good example of a song with a shuffle rhythm. Watch out for the $\frac{2}{4}$ measure. This is a measure of music that contains only two beats instead of the usual four.

Revolution
Words and Music by John Lennon and Paul McCartney

shuffle rhythm

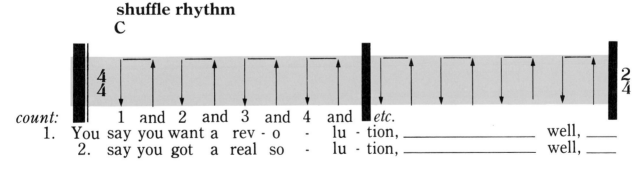

count:
1. You say you want a rev-o-lu-tion, _____ well, ____
2. say you got a real so-lu-tion, _____ well, ____

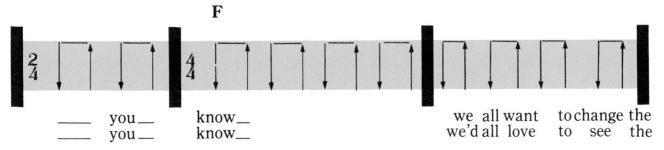

_____ you_ know_
_____ you_ know_

we all want to change the
we'd all love to see the

Revolution *continued*

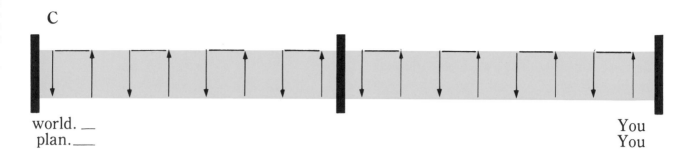

C

world. __
plan. __

You
You

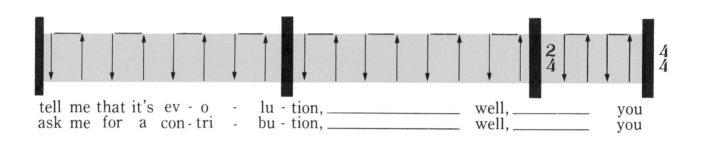

tell me that it's ev - o - lu - tion, _____ well, _____ you
ask me for a con - tri - bu - tion, _____ well, _____ you

F

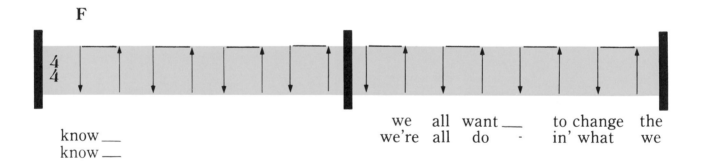

we all want __ to change the
we're all do - in' what we

know __
know __

G7

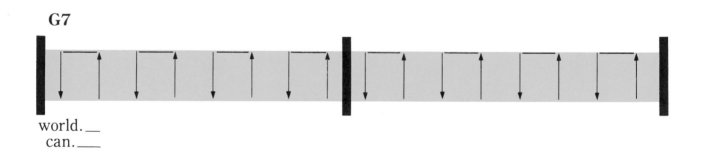

world. __
can. __

Am
G

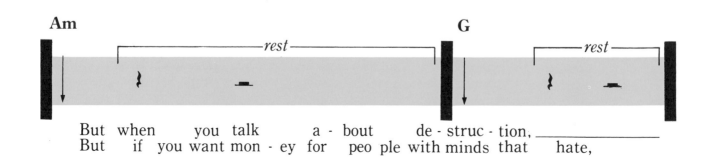

But when you talk a - bout de - struc - tion, _____
But if you want mon - ey for peo ple with minds that hate,

28

Revolution *continued*

Am

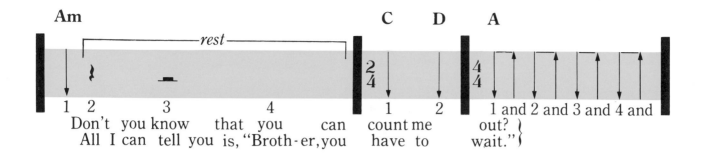

rest

1 2 3 4

Don't you know that you can count me out? }
All I can tell you is, "Broth-er, you have to wait." }

C   D   A

1 and 2 and 3 and 4 and

G

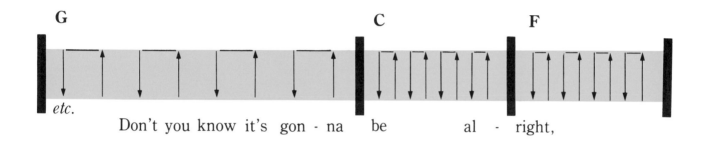

etc.

Don't you know it's gon - na be al - right,

C   F

C

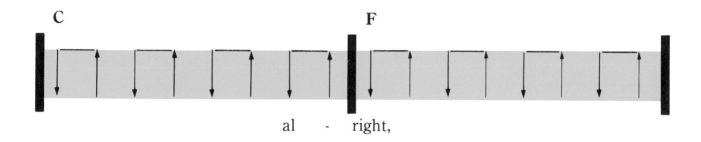

al - right,

F

C

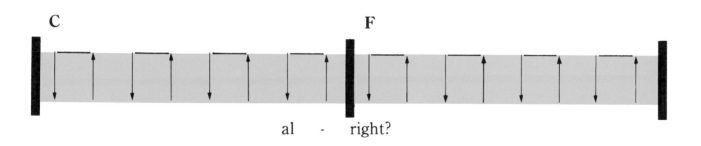

al - right?

F

G

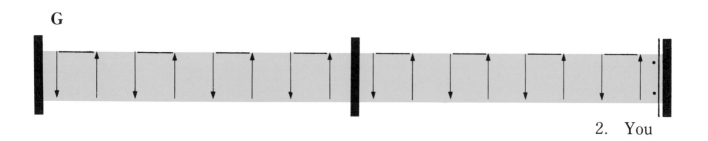

2. You

Closing Comments

That's it for now. Once you have a grasp of the basics that we've covered in **Books 1** and **2**, you'll be all set for the more advanced material we'll cover in **Books 3** and **4**, such as bar chords, specialty chords, soloing, more riffs, and playing up the neck. See you then!

The Complete Rock Guitar Player.

by Steve Tarshis.

Book Three.

Amsco Publications
New York/London/Sydney/Cologne

Contents

The Songs

About This Book

Welcome to **Book 3** of the **Complete Rock Guitar Player**. At this point you should be able to play the open-position chords we've covered so far, and you should be using them to play the songs we've gone over and even some songs you've picked up on your own. I want to begin by showing you some new chords in open position. (Open-position chords are chords that use open strings and that are played on the first few frets of the guitar.) The chords that I'm about to show you will begin to move your guitar playing away from the basics and into some of the special kinds of sounds that are essential to rock guitar playing.

Ziggy Stardust

I want you to find a copy of David Bowie's "Ziggy Stardust" and listen to the opening lick. Here are the chords that we're going to use to play this lick:

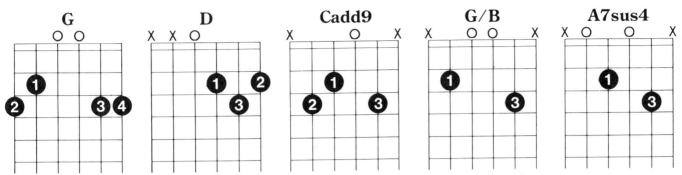

G D Cadd9 G/B A7sus4

The **D** chord should be familiar to you from Books 1 and 2, but notice that we are playing the **G** chord in a slightly different way, using the third and fourth fingers on the **B** and **E** strings. This voicing will give us a stronger sound than that of the other **G** chord. The **Cadd9** chord adds the note D to the usual C chord. G/B is read as "G over B," and it means that a G chord is to be played with the note B as the lowest note. (The note B should also be played by the bass player when he sees this chord symbol.) Notice that all of these chords are played with the third finger on the third fret of the second string. This finger should not be moved at all as you move from chord to chord.

Play these chords, and then try this opening lick from Bowie's "Ziggy Stardust," as written below in standard notation and tablature.

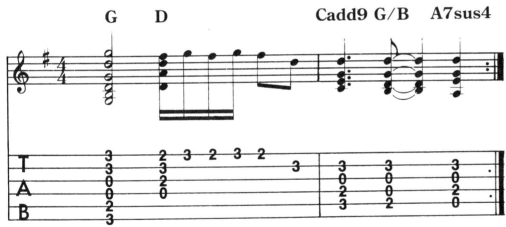

G D Cadd9 G/B A7sus4

Notice the melody that's played over the D chord in the second half of the first measure. Hold the D chord and play the G notes (third fret of the first string) with your pinky, lifting it on and off. The last two notes in the first measure are part of the D chord, so just pick these notes while holding onto the chord.

Now let's go on to the verse of this song. To play the verse, we will use a combination of chords and licks. First, I want to show you your first *bar chord:* **B minor**. One of the reasons we use bar chords is to achieve a fuller and more complete sound. Notice that your first finger must bar across the second fret covering the first five strings. Don't be surprised if this chord is hard to play at first. Keep at it and soon you'll get used to it.

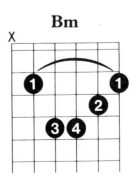

Bm

Now that you've advanced a bit on the guitar, you should be able to make up some of your own strums based on the patterns that we've covered in Books 1 and 2. In the music to the verse of "Ziggy Stardust" below, you will see rhythm slashes (for strumming) and also some notation to indi-cate riffs. Use the chord symbols above the slashes to tell you what chord to finger. In this way you can play both "rhythm" and "lead" guitar at the same time. If you prefer, play only the chords, or only the lead part.

Ziggy Stardust
Words and Music by David Bowie

After two verses of "Ziggy Stardust," each having the same music, we hear a different section. Before you play this section, I want to tell you about a very important concept in rock guitar playing: the **power chord.** A power chord, as the word implies, is used when we want a heavier sound than that provided by the chords we have learned so far. Power chords use only the low strings of the guitar, leaving out the third of the chord and playing only the root and the fifth. These chords may be moved freely around the neck. The diagram below shows the fingering for an **A** power chord. We will use the notation **A5** to indicate an **A** power chord.

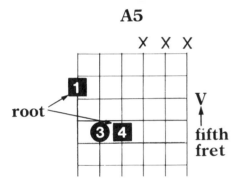

A5

root

V
↑
fifth
fret

Notice that this chord is played at the fifth fret. The chord gets its name from the note that has a square around it in the diagram. This note is the *root* of the chord. We can shift this fingering to any fret on the neck, producing different chords. The name of the chord will change as the root of the chord moves up and down the neck. For example, the power-chord fingering played at the third fret will give us a **G5** chord. The same power-chord fingering played at the first fret will give us an **F5** chord.

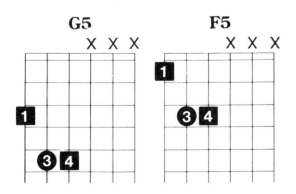

G5   **F5**

It is important to realize that the reason these chords can be moved around the neck is that no open strings are involved. This happens quite naturally. As your first finger comes across the neck to play the note on the sixth string, allow it to touch the first three strings lightly enough to stop them from sounding. This way, only the three low strings will produce notes and you can strum freely without worrying about hitting open strings.

The music below shows the chords to the section of "Ziggy Stardust" that uses power chords. Use all downstrokes to get a powerful sound. When you get to the **F5** chord you will notice that a lick is played "within the chord." While you are holding the **F5** chord, lift the first finger to sound the open **E**, put the finger back down to play the **F**, then repeat this motion to play the lick "within the chord." Play the **D** and **Em** chords in the usual way in open position.

Ziggy Stardust *continued*

The Chromatic Scale

To be a proficient rock guitarist, you must be able to play power chords anywhere on the neck. As we have seen, this is just a matter of being able to name the root of each chord. In the power chords we have just learned, the root is always played with the first finger on the low **E** string. For this reason you will want to learn the names of all the notes on the sixth string.

To help you accomplish this, I want to talk a little more about music theory—specifically, the **chromatic scale.** If you put your finger anywhere on a piano keyboard and play all the black and white notes in order, you will be playing the chromatic scale. Similarly, if you put your finger on any string of the guitar and play each fret in order, you will also be playing the chromatic scale.

As you know, the musical alphabet utilizes the letters **A** through **G**. However, the musical alphabet also makes use of sharps and flats. Between every two letters there exists another note. This note has two names—a sharp name and a flat name. There are two exceptions. Between the notes **B** and **C** and between the notes **E** and **F** there is no other note. I've written the chromatic scale below. As you can see, every sharp name also has a flat name. Either one can be used, depending on what key we are in.

A   A# or B♭   B   C   C# or D♭   D   D# or E♭   E   F   F# or G♭   G   G# or A♭   A

The distance between any two adjacent notes in the chromatic scale is called a **half step.** On your guitar, the distance from one fret to the next is a half step. The sixth string, when played open, sounds the note **E.** The first fret sounds **F** (one half-step above **E**). The second fret sounds **F#** or **G♭** (another half step higher). We can keep going and name all the notes on the sixth string, as shown in the chart below.

Notes on the Sixth String

Fret	Note Name
open	E
1	F
2	F# or G♭
3	G
4	G# or A♭
5	A
6	A# or B♭
7	B
8	C
9	C# or D♭
10	D
11	D# or E♭
12	E

Notice that the note on twelfth fret has the same name as the open string (both are **E**). Likewise, the thirteenth-fret note has the same name as the one on the first fret, the fourteenth the same as the second, and so on.

Now let's put this information to use. Suppose we want to play a **D** power chord. According to the chart, the note **D** is on the tenth fret of the sixth string. We know that the root of the **D** chord is played with the first finger on the sixth string, so to play the **D** power chord, just move the power-chord fingering to tenth position. (Positions on the guitar are named according to which fret the first finger covers.) To play an **F#** power chord, move the fingering to the second fret (second position). To play an **A♭** power chord, move to the fourth position, and so on.

9

You Really Got Me

Let's use this new information to play a real rock-and-roll standard, the Kinks' "You Really Got Me." To play this song, we will use our power-chord fingering to play a **G5** chord in third position, an **A5** chord in fifth position, a **B5** chord in seventh position, a **D5** chord in tenth position,

and an **E5** chord in twelfth position. In this way we can play an entire song with five chords, using only one fingering. Remember, the number **5** signifies a power chord. In the chord diagrams below, a square around a number indicates the root of the chord.

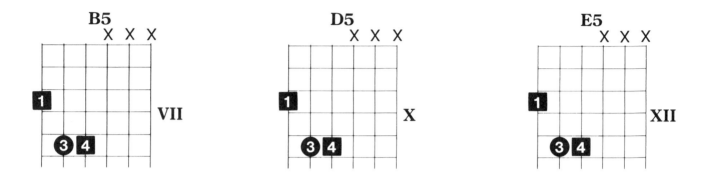

Use all down strokes to get a powerful sound when you play "You Really Got Me."

You Really Got Me
Words and Music by Ray Davies

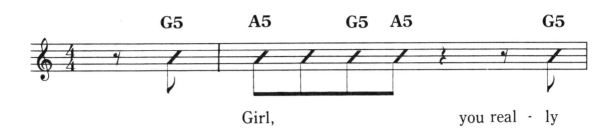

Girl,   you real - ly

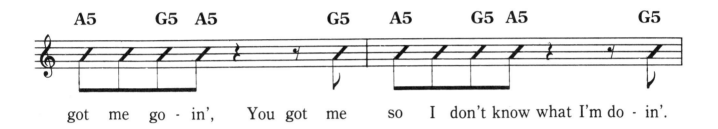

got me go - in', You got me so I don't know what I'm do - in'.

Yeah,   you real - ly

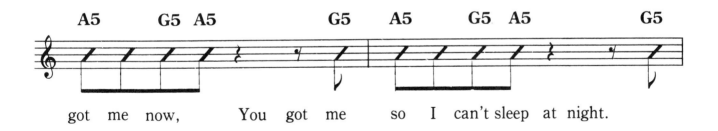

got me now, You got me so I can't sleep at night.

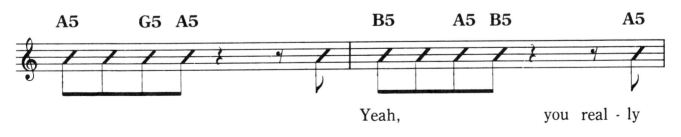

Yeah,   you real - ly

You Really Got Me *continued*

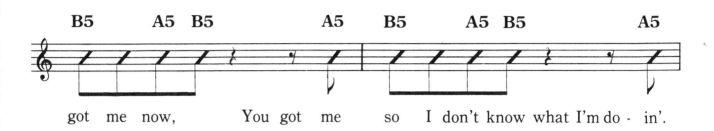

got me now, You got me so I don't know what I'm do - in'.

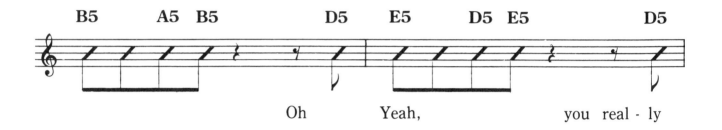

Oh Yeah, you real - ly

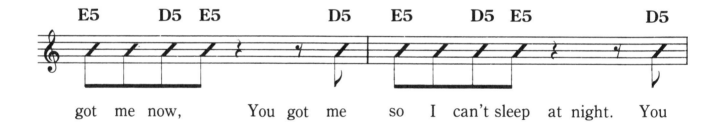

got me now, You got me so I can't sleep at night. You

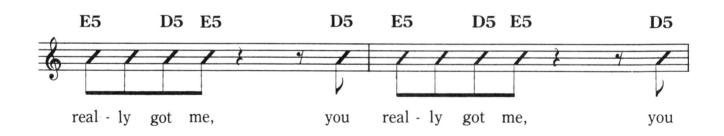

real - ly got me, you real - ly got me, you

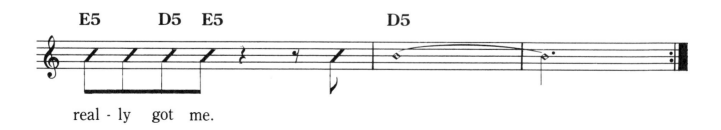

real - ly got me.

The E Shape Bar Chord

Now that you've worked a little with moveable fingerings, I want to introduce you to another important fingering or "shape." Actually, the power-chord shape that you now know is part of a larger shape, the "E shape" bar chord. An example of an E shape bar chord is pictured in the diagram below.

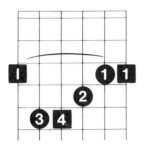

You will notice that the second, third, and fourth, fingers outline a shape that is the same as an **E** chord in first position. The first finger forms a "bar" that allows this sound to be moved up the neck. The first finger on the sixth string plays the root of the chord, as it does for the power chord. The name of the E shape bar chord will be the same as the name of the note the first finger is playing on the sixth string. When this shape is played at the fifth fret, for example, the chord will be an **A** chord. Likewise, in seventh position the chord will be a **B** chord, and at the first fret, an **F** chord.

I Wanna Be Sedated

We are going to use this bar chord shape to play the Ramones' "I Wanna Be Sedated." To play this song we will use the open-position E chord and the **A** and **B** bar chords. Play **A** as an E shape bar chord in fifth position and **B** as an E shape bar chord in seventh position, as shown in the chord diagrams below.

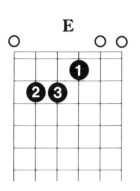

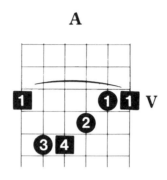

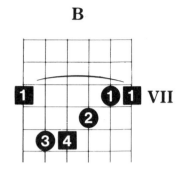

Play this song with a straight-ahead down-up rhythm, as indicated in the music below. The strum I've written out in the first measure is the one you should use for the whole song.

I Wanna Be Sedated
Words and Music by The Ramones

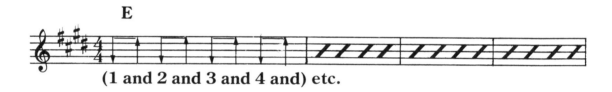

(1 and 2 and 3 and 4 and) etc.

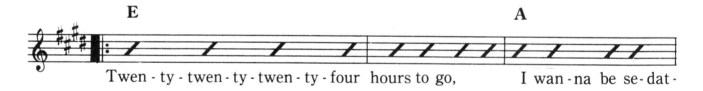

Twen - ty - twen - ty - twen - ty - four hours to go, I wan - na be se - dat -

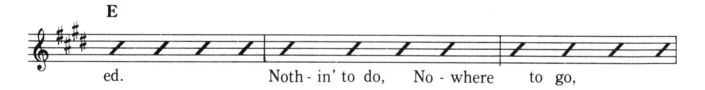

ed. Noth - in' to do, No - where to go,

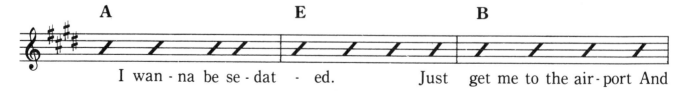

I wan - na be se - dat - ed. Just get me to the air - port And

put me on a plane. Hur - ry, hur - ry, hur - ry, be - fore I go in - sane. I

can't con - trol my fin - gers, I can't con - trol my brain. Oh no oh oh oh

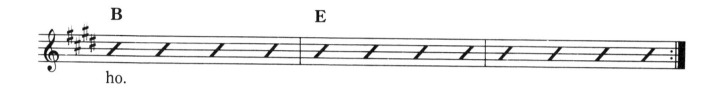

ho.

This verse is played twice, and then there is a guitar solo section which uses the

same chords, but in a different pattern, as shown below.

After the guitar solo, we hear two more verses. But if you listen to the record, you will hear that the key has gone up from **E** to **F♯**. A change of key like this is called a

modulation. Playing in the new key will give you a chance to practice more bar chords. The new ones are written below.

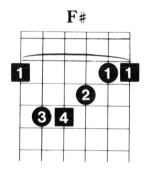

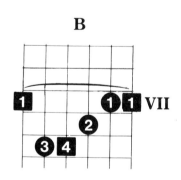

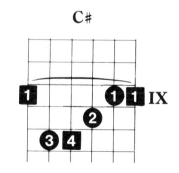

I Wanna Be Sedated *continued*

Here's the rest of the song in the new key of **F#**.

There's only one small section left in this song, the **tag.** A tag is a repeated section at the end of a song. The tag to "I Wanna Be Sedated" goes like this:

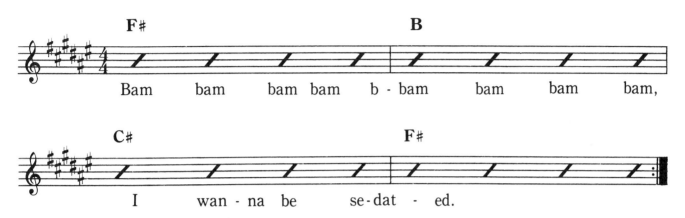

F#   B

Bam   bam   bam bam   b - bam   bam   bam   bam,

C#   F#

I   wan - na   be   se - dat - ed.

E Minor Shape Bar Chords

We have seen that the E shape bar chord allows us to play all the major chords by moving one fingering up and down the neck. Now we're going to see how to do the same thing with the minor chords. Below you will see diagrams for the two E shape bar chords—one for major and one for minor. As you can see, if you finger the major bar chord and then lift your second finger, you will have the minor bar chord fingering.

The following chart shows the location on the neck of all the E shape and E minor shape bar chords. Notice that when we speak of a specific major chord, we name only the root. For example, a **D** chord is understood to be a major chord. Chord symbols that refer to minor chords, however, must contain the word "minor," or the abbreviation "min" or "m." So, **E, A, Db, F#,** etc., all refer to major chords. Minor chords would be named **Em, Am, Db, F#,** etc.

E Major Shape   E Minor Shape

Again, knowing the names of the notes on the sixth string is the key to knowing where all the minor bar chords are found on the neck. To play an **A minor** chord for example, finger the E minor shape bar chord at the fifth fret. To play a **C minor** chord, finger this shape at the eighth fret.

Fret	E Shape Bar Chord	E Minor Shape Bar Chord
open	E	Em
1	F	Fm
2	F# or Gb	F#m or Gbm
3	G	Gm
4	G# or Ab	G#m or Abm
5	A	Am
6	A# or Bb	A#m or Bbm
7	B	Bm
8	C	Cm
9	C# or Db	C#m or Dbm
10	D	Dm
11	D# or Eb	D#m or Ebm
12	E	Em

Am   Cm

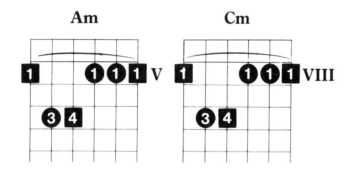

18

Runaway

We're going to use the E shape bar chords to play "Runaway." This song was a hit in the sixties for Del Shanon and has been covered several times since. The chart below shows the chords you will need.

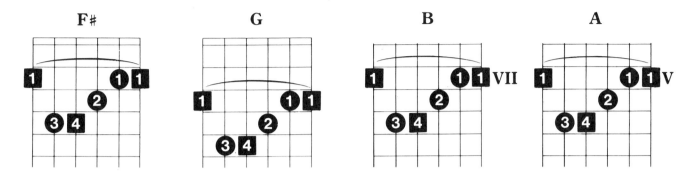

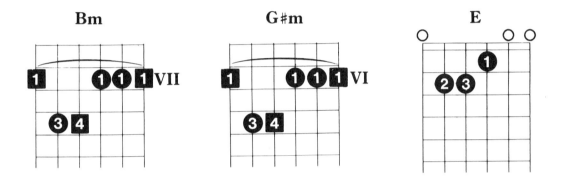

This is a good song to practice your major and minor bar chords on. You will find that as soon as you are able to get a good sound out of these bar chord shapes, songs like this become just a matter of moving your left hand to the correct frets, and playing either the major or minor E shape bar chord. (In **Book 4**, we'll add another shape so you won't have to move your left hand up and down the neck so much.) I've written out "Runaway" with a simple down, down, down-up, down-up strum, but I hope that you're experimenting with your own strumming patterns at this point.

Runaway
Words and Music by Del Shannon and Max Crook

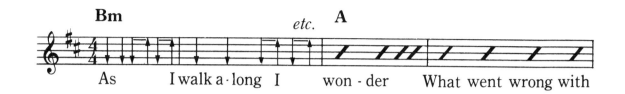

As I walk a·long I won·der What went wrong with

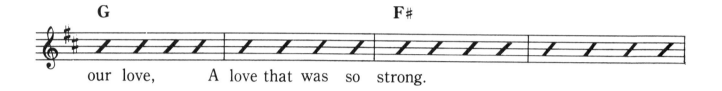

our love, A love that was so strong.

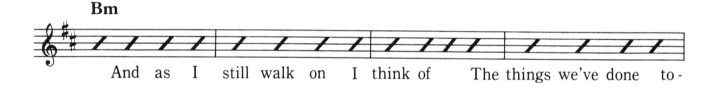

And as I still walk on I think of The things we've done to-

geth·er While our hearts were young;

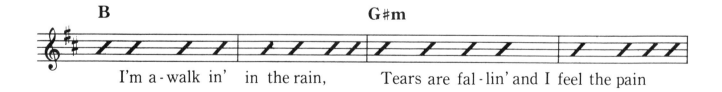

I'm a·walk in' in the rain, Tears are fal·lin' and I feel the pain

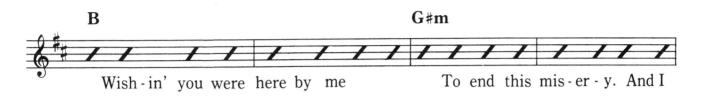

B   **G♯m**

Wish-in' you were here by me   To end this mis-er-y. And I

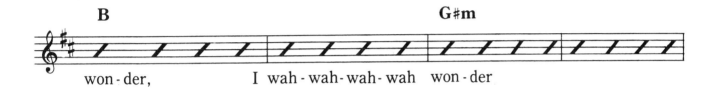

B   **G♯m**

won-der,   I wah-wah-wah-wah won-der

B   **G♯m**

Why,   why, why, why, why, why she ran a-way.   And I

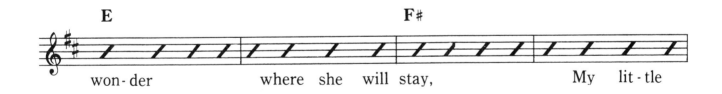

E   **F♯**

won-der   where she will stay,   My lit-tle

B   **E**   **B**   **F♯**

run-a-way   a-run-run-run-run run-a-way.

More Moveable Forms: The Chuck Berry Riff

Remember the Chuck Berry riff in open position that you learned in **Book 1**? Now you're going to learn to play this riff as a moveable shape so that you can play it anywhere on the neck, in any key. The diagram below shows this shape at the third fret. As you can see, the root, which has a square around it, is played with the first finger on the sixth string. This is the same finger and string used to play E and E minor shape bar chords. You're probably beginning to see how important it is to know the names of the notes on the sixth string, and I hope you're beginning to memorize them. Notice that the fourth finger (pinky) is shown in parentheses. This is to indicate that the fourth finger will be going on and off this note.

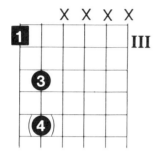

To play this riff, play only the low E and A strings. Play two downstrokes with the pinky off, then two downstrokes with the pinky on. This sequence is repeated as many times as necessary, depending on the song you are playing. The music below shows four measures of this riff in G.

This may not be easy for you at first, especially when you are playing on the lower part of the neck where the frets are wider. You're giving your fourth finger a good stretch, and it may take you a while to get used to it. But the effort will be well worth it because this is one of the most important rhythm patterns in rock guitar playing.

The Chuck Berry riff is often used as a **substitute chord.** For example, instead of playing an **A** or **A7** chord, a guitarist will substitute the Chuck Berry riff in **A** to get a sound that rocks more. For the most part, the Chuck Berry riff is substituted only for major and dominant seventh chords.

Blues

You may have heard musicians speak of a **twelve-bar blues progression.** The word *blues* means many things to many people, but here we're using it to mean a very specific kind of chord progression. This chord progression is so imbedded in our musical tradition that any musician worthy of the name knows how to play it in every key. Besides being the basis of many rock-and-roll songs (such as "Johnny B. Goode"), the twelve-bar blues progression is the one players most often use to jam together. If you can play blues, you can jam with most other musicians.

The music below shows the basic twelve-bar blues progression in the key of **A**.

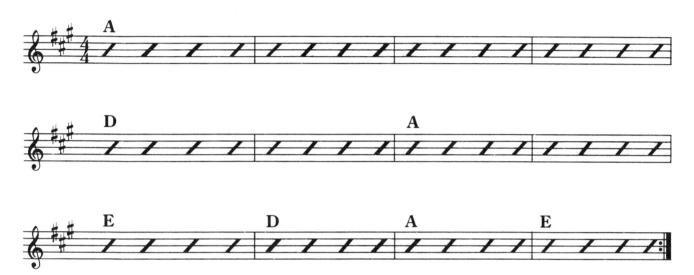

A tried-and-true method of playing this progression is to use the Chuck Berry riff to play all the chords. To play the twelve-bar blues in the key of **A**, we'll be playing the riff at the fifth fret for the **A** chord, the tenth fret for the **D** chord, and the twelfth fret for the **E** chord, as you can see in the diagrams below.

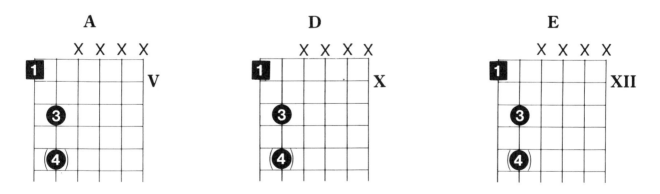

Remember, when you play these forms pick only the low **E** and **A** strings and use only downstrokes. The music below shows the twelve-bar blues progression in **A**, played with the Chuck Berry riff. I call this the "All-Purpose Blues."

All-Purpose Blues (Background)

Music by Steve Tarshis

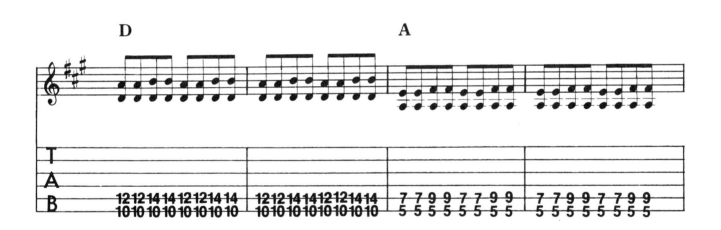

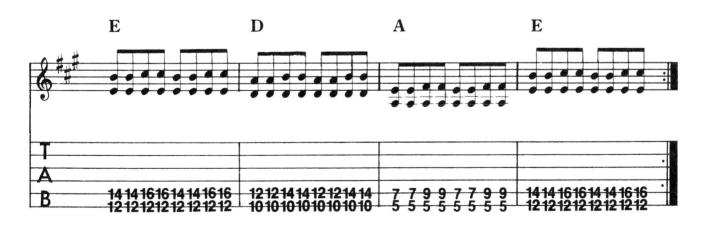

Blues Soloing

I've been referring to musicans **jamming** on the twelve-bar blues progression. You might already realize that this means that the players are **improvising.** The lead guitarist is making up melodic lines to go along with the chords.

A good way to start talking about blues soloing is with a discussion of scales. For the improviser, scales provide note choices. If we know that a certain scale works well with certain chords, then playing notes from that scale while the chords are in the background will, at the very least, give us lines that sound "correct." Playing the right scale assures you that you won't play any really "wrong" notes, and allows you to concentrate on finding great notes.

Shown below is a diagram of the **A blues scale**. Every **A** note (the root of the scale) has a square around it. This scale is also known as the **minor pentatonic scale**. It provides the notes that work well with the twelve-bar blues progression in the key of **A**. Although it is called the blues scale, its use is not restricted to blues. In fact, it is the scale most used in rock soloing.

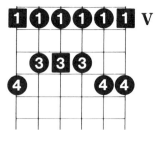

Although the diagram above looks like a chord chart, it is not a chord, but rather a scale—and the notes should be played one at a time. Start on the low E string, and play the note at the fifth fret, then the note at the eighth fret. Now go to the fifth string and play the note at the fifth fret, then the note at the seventh fret, and so on until all the notes are played. Then, play all the notes in reverse order, highest to lowest. Repeat this several times to get the feel of this scale. Notice that the **A** blues scale is played in the same position (fifth position) as the **A** bar chord, the **A** power chord, and the **A** Chuck Berry riff. I've written out the notes in their correct sequence below.

The **A** blues scale is the scale that guitarists use to "jam" on the twelve-bar blues progression in **A**. All the notes in the scale sound "right" against all the chords. Of course, it takes more than playing just the "right" notes to make a good solo, but knowing these notes will take you a long way in the right direction.

To help you get started I've written out a solo you can play against the "All-Purpose Blues" progression. This solo will also illustrate some of the important **articulations** that rock guitarists use. Articulations are effects used when playing individual notes, such as **bends** and **vibrato.** A bend is played by fingering a note and pushing the string up until the pitch of the note changes. Vibrato is produced by moving the finger rapidly while fingering a note in order to make the pitch waver or shake. We'll be examining these articulations in detail as we go on.

The following solo is based on the notes of the **A** blues scale and should be played against the chords of an **A** blues progression, such as "All-Purpose Blues."

All-Purpose Blues (Solo)
Music by Steve Tarshis

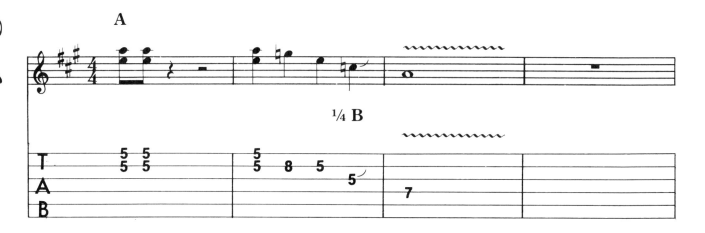

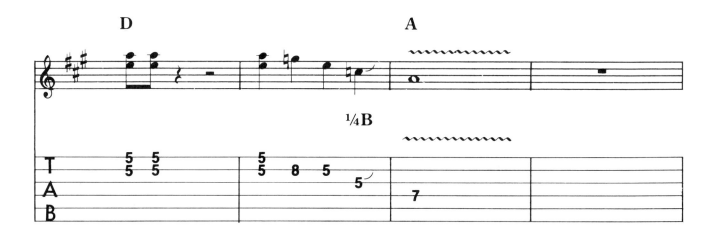

You will notice that this solo is made up of one phrase that is played twice, a variation, and then another repeat of the first phrase. In the last measure there is a riff that will lead you back for a repeat of the solo (or a new solo that you might make up yourself). This ending riff is called a **turnaround.**

In the second, sixth, and tenth measures you will see the symbol ¼ **B**. This indicates a **quarter bend**. To play this bend, put your finger on the note (**C** on the fifth fret of the third string) and push it up slightly—not enough to move to the next pitch, but enough to hear a difference. This is a quarter bend and it is used to play a "blue" note. This is a very important effect for playing blues and rock-and-roll leads.

In the third, seventh, and eleventh measures you will see a wavy line over the note (**A** on the seventh fret of the fourth string). This symbol tells you to play that note with vibrato. To produce vibrato, play the note and then move your finger up and down slightly so that you hear the pitch waver. Guitarists use this effect quite often on long notes.

After you have learned this solo, you might want to try making up your own solos based on the blues scale. Creating a solo is a real skill, and you will need to do a lot of listening and practicing to get the hang of it, but this should start you on your way.

Closing Comments

We've covered a lot of ground and you should be noticing a marked improvement in your rock guitar playing. By using the concepts and techniques you've learned here you can start to figure out songs on your own, jam with friends, and begin to develop your personal rock and roll style.

Keep practicing, and I'll see you in **Book 4!**

The Complete Rock Guitar Player.

by Steve Tarshis.

Book Four.

Amsco Publications
New York/London/Sydney/Cologne

Contents

The Songs

About This Book

We've made quite a bit of progress since **Book 1**, and I congratulate you. Keep working as hard as you have been, because the time you spend practicing will always pay off. In **Book 4**, I hope to start you on your way to sounding "real" — like someone playing in a band or on a record. We'll be talking about some of the most advanced techniques you'll need if you're going to play in a rock band. We'll be covering riffs, lead guitar techniques, and some more bar chords.

Mannish Boy

Before we continue our work on bar chords, I want to talk some more about open-position chords. Many blues and rock songs are in the key of **E**. Chords in this key are often played in open position. Also, there are certain riffs that guitarists use over and over when playing in **E**.

The riff we're going to learn now was developed by the great Chicago bluesmen and is strongly associated with Muddy Waters and Bo Diddley. We're going to use the riff to play Muddy's classic, "Mannish Boy." You can also hear this type of lick in Muddy Waters's "Hoochie Coochie Man," Bo Diddley's "I'm a Man," and many other tunes.

(E7)

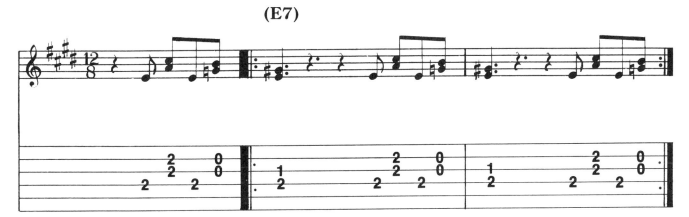

As you get deeper into rock guitar, you wil discover that a lot of "lead guitar" playing involves playing chords in ways that go beyond just strumming conventional shapes. For example, the Muddy Waters riff above is used as an alternative to strumming an E7 chord. In the song "Mannish Boy," the entire band plays this riff, and Muddy sings the words as a response to the band, like this:

Mannish Boy

Words and Music by McKinley Morganfield, Ellis McDaniel & Mel London

Now, when I was a young boy,

at the age of five,　　My mother said, "He'll be

the greatest man alive."　　But now I'm a man,

a male, twenty-one.　　I want you to believe me honey,

we havin' lots of fun.   I'm a man.

I spell   "M,"   "A," child,

"N."   *(etc.)*

In **Book 3** we began to talk about soloing using the blues scale in the key of **A**. Now let's talk about soloing against the Muddy Waters riff using the **E** blues scale. This scale is similar to the **A** blues scale, but when playing the **E** blues scale, open strings are used. The diagram and the music below show the E blues scale. When playing the notes in the diagram, don't forget that the circles on top indicate that the open strings are part of the scale.

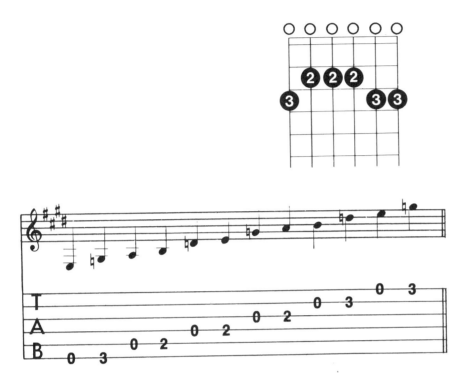

If you can, play the Muddy Waters riff into a cassette recorder, or have another guitarist play the riff. Then, listen to the way the scale sounds against the riff. All the notes should sound "right." However, to play a "real" sounding solo, we must learn how to combine the individual notes in the scale into melodic fragments. We have to learn some "licks." You can think of the notes of a scale as letters that must be combined into words in order to tell a story.

The first lick we're going to learn uses a technique called a **hammeron.** To play the hammeron below, pick the open **D** string, and then quickly fret the string at the second fret with your second finger. If you do this move correctly, you'll understand why it's called a hammeron. The left-hand finger acts like a hammer hitting the string to produce a second note after the first note has sounded. The overall effect is to produce two notes while picking only one with the right hand.

A hammeron is indicated in the tablature by the letter **H**.

Do you remember the 1/4 bend from **Book 3**? We're going to use it again, but this time on the low **E** string. Because this bend is on the sixth string, we're going to bend the string down (toward the **A** string) instead of up so that the string doesn't go off the neck. This next lick has a 1/4 bend on the third fret of the sixth string followed by the open **E**.

Another of the important effects you'll need for playing lead guitar is the **pulloff.** To play a pulloff, finger a note (in this case the third fret of the first string), pick the note, and then scrape the left-hand finger off the string producing a second tone. The left-hand finger acts like a pick.

A pulloff is indicated by the letter **P**, as in the example below.

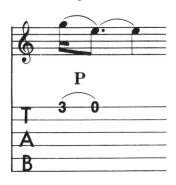

I want to show you one more lick, and then we'll learn a solo to play over the Muddy Waters riff. It's important to understand that these licks are not isolated examples that you'll use only in this one tune. These licks should become part of a "vocabulary" that you'll be using all the time, whenever you want to "speak" lead guitar.

This lick uses an effect called the **reverse bend.** Finger the second fret of the third string and play a 1/4 bend. (Remember, a 1/4 bend changes the pitch, but not enough to hear the next higher tone.) Next, release that bend. This is a reverse bend. Finally sound the open G by playing a pulloff. You've picked only one note, but three pitches have sounded: the 1/4 bend, the reverse bend, and the pulloff. Even though it takes a while to explain, the actual lick should be played rapidly. Notice that the number **3** is written over the eighth notes. This means that this is an **eighth-note triplet**: three evenly spaced notes to be played within one beat.

A reverse bend is indicated by the letter **R**, as in the example below.

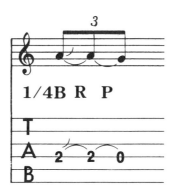

We are going to put these licks together to play a solo over the Muddy Waters riff. The "call and response" structure is the same as if there were a singer, but instead of a singer, a lead guitartist (you!) is taking a solo. You can see in the music below that the middle of every measure is left empty. This is to leave space for your lead guitar licks.

Practice the following solo until you feel comfortable with it, and then try it against the Muddy Water riff (played back on the cassette you recorded or played by another guitarist). As soon as you can you should start trying to make up your own licks based on the **E** blues scale. It will help you to listen to other guitarists. You'll find that licks developed by bluesmen like Robert Johnson, Muddy Waters, Elmore James, B.B. King, and Albert King have formed the basis for the playing of Jimi Hendrix, Eric Clapton, Jimmy Page, and so many other rock guitar players. A careful study of the blues is essential to good rock guitar playing.

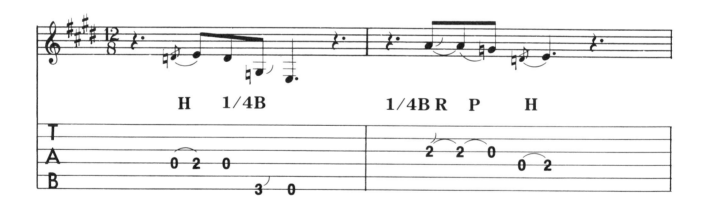

Back in Black

I think you'll see the connection between blues and rock when we take a look at AC/DC's "Back in Black." The riff from "Back in Black" is one of the most distinctive metal signatures in rock. You know right away what tune this is from the opening measures. A combination of chords and licks is used. The chords are power chords similar to the ones we saw in **Book 3**. Here, however, they are played in open position. The three power chords used are shown below.

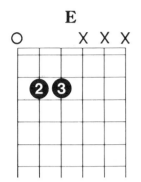

E

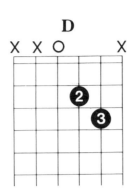

D

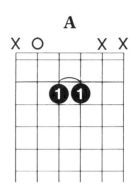

A

Power chords, as we have seen, are used as substitute chords to get a more powerful sound. The key to playing these open-position power chords is to play only the strings that are indicated in the diagram. Do not play the strings with **X**'s over them.

The **E-D-A** pattern alternates with two single-note riffs. The first is a blues riff from the **E** blues scale. The second is a low-note riff that can be heard in many R&B tunes. Look at the first lick below. When you play the bend, you must bend the note **A** a whole step to **B** (shown in parentheses). The second finger plays the second fret of the third string and bends until the **sound** of the note on the fourth fret of the third string is heard. The finger does not change frets. The note is then let back down (reverse bend), and finally the open G is sounded with a pulloff. It sounds a lot more complicated than it really is. I hope you have a copy of the record to help you work it out. A little practice is all it takes.

Now let's put it all together. The following four-measure phrase is played twice, forming the intro to "Back in Black."

Back in Black
Words and Music by Angus Young, Malcolm Young, Brian Johnson

The verse to "Back in Black" uses the same riff as the intro as shown below.

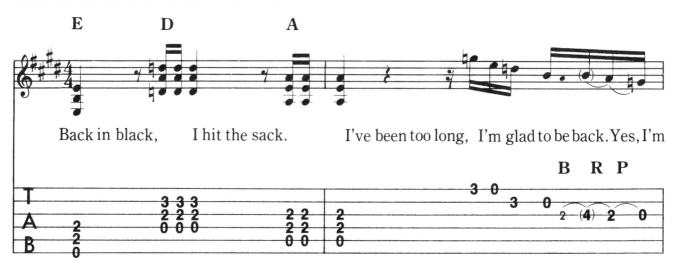

Back in black, I hit the sack. I've been too long, I'm glad to be back. Yes, I'm

let loose, from the noose that's kept me hangin' about. I keep

lookin' at the sky 'cause it's gettin' me high. Forget the hearse 'cause I'll never die. I got

nine lives, cat's eyes, abusin' every one of them and runnin' wild.

I'm going to show you the chorus section of "Back in Black," but first we need to do some more work on power chords. In **Book 3** we covered power chords with a sixth-string root, and in this book we've looked at some power chords in open position. It's time now to cover the power chords with a fifth-string root. With the addition of these chords you'll know most of the power chords you'll need for playing hard rock and heavy metal.

In **Book 3** we covered the chromatic scale, the scale that names all the notes in order. We're going to use this scale to name all the notes on the fifth (**A**) string because these notes will be the roots of the A shape power chords. The following chart shows the names of the notes on the fifth string.

Notes on the Fifth String

Fret	Note Name
Open	A
1	A♯ or B♭
2	B
3	C
4	C♯ or D♭
5	D
6	D♯ or E♭
7	E
8	F
9	F♯ or G♭
10	G
11	G♯ or A♭
12	A

Notice that the twelfth fret is the same as the open string (both are **A**). Likewise, the thirteenth fret is the same as the first fret, the fourteenth the same as the second fret, and so on.

In the diagram below you will see the A shape power chord. The actual name of the chord depends on which note is being played on the fifth string. If you play this shape with your first finger on the second fret, it will be a **B** power chord. As in **Book 3**, we will indicate this with the chord symbol **B5**. Play the shape at the fifth fret and it will be **D5** chord; at the seventh fret it will be an **E5** chord, and so on.

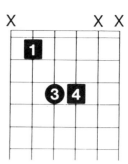

It is important to remember that this is a moveable chord form, and like all moveable forms, it uses no open strings. When playing this shape you must be careful to play only those notes that are fingered. This becomes easier to do if you **mute** the strings that are not to be played. To mute a string, cover it with a finger of your left hand with enough pressure to block the sound but not enough pressure to cause a note to sound. When playing the A shape power chord, the tip of the first finger mutes the sixth string while the bottom of the first finger mutes the first and second strings. Once muted, these strings will not produce any sound even if the right hand strikes them. The right hand may then strum without being inhibited by having to play only a few strings. Don't worry if this technique seems too advanced for you right now. Keep trying, and eventually it will become second nature.

I want to show you one other chord that we need in order to play the chorus of "Back in Black." This chord is a **small-note voicing.** Small-note voicings are smaller versions of chords you already know. The power chords that we have learned are good examples of small note voicings. Rock guitarists frequently use these kinds of chords to play *parts*. Playing parts means playing riffs, melodies, and small-note voicings instead of just strumming chords. This is essentially what a rock guitar player does in a band. It's his special way of orchestrating the music.

This next chord is based on the E shape bar chord we learned in **Book 3**. It is a **G** chord with the root on the sixth string, *even though this string is not played*. Below, I have diagrammed this chord, which is played in third position, and the bar chord that it is a part of. Play the two chords and you will see that the notes are the same except that in the small-note voicing the sixth and fifth strings have been omitted.

It is important to remember that the name of this chord comes from the note on the sixth string, even when this note is not played.

In the music below, notice how the guitar part is a combination of licks and small-note voicings. This kind of part is very effective. I know it may be difficult for you to play this up to speed, but I want you to work on it because this kind of part is what guitarists are really playing on records and on stage.

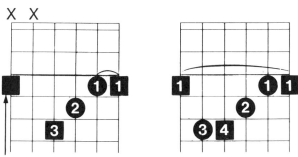

Think of this note as the root even though it is not played.

Back in Black *continued*

The A Shape Bar Chord

The chart below shows the name of A shape bar chord at each fret. It will be the same chord name as the A shape power chord, which is derived from the A shape bar chord.

Fret	Chord Name
open	A
1	A♯ or B♭
2	B
3	C
4	C♯ or D♭
5	D
6	D♯ or E♭
7	E
8	F
9	F♯ or G♭
10	G
11	G♯ or A♭
12	A

As with all other moveable chord shapes, the chord at the thirteenth fret has the same name as the chord at the first fret, the chord at the fourteenth fret has the same name as the chord at the second fret, and so on.

Let's leave open position for a while and talk some more about bar chords. In **Book 3** we learned the E shape bar chord. This is one of the two main bar chord shapes used by rock guitarists. The other is the **A shape bar chord**.

This chord gets its name from the note that is played on the fifth (**A**) string. If you play this shape with your first finger on the second fret, it will be a **B** chord. Play the shape at the fifth fret and it will be a **D** chord. At the seventh fret it will be an **E** chord, and so on. Try this chord at the seventh fret. If you're having trouble getting a good sound, tilt your wrist slightly, putting more pressure on the third finger. Your third finger should be touching the first string enough to mute it, but not enough to sound a note. The tip of the first finger should touch the low **E** string so that it doesn't sound. Play the shape at different frets to get a feel for it. This shape may take some getting used to, but you'll want to get it down because it is one of the most important chord shapes in rock guitar playing.

The following are typical chords that you might find in a song that uses A shape bar chords.

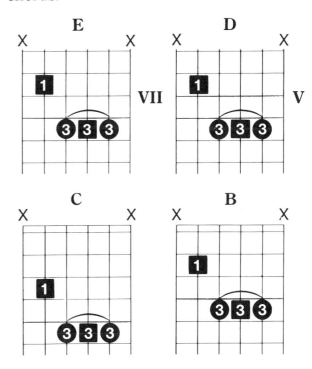

17

Play through the chord progression below to help you get used to playing A shape bar chords. Use a simple strum of one chord per beat. Then make up some more complex strumming rhythms after you feel comfortable with the chords.

E   D   C   B

From the A shape bar chord we also can derive the **A minor shape bar chord**. It looks like this:

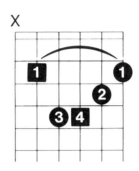

We have seen this chord before. At the second fret it is a B minor chord, at the third fret a C minor chord, and at the seventh fret an E minor chord, as shown below.

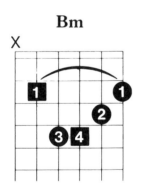
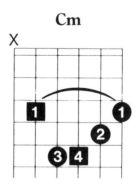
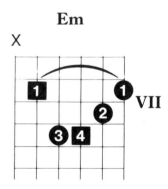

Bm   **Cm**   **Em**

Like the other A shape chords, the name of the chord comes from the note played on the fifth string.

The chart below shows all of the major, minor, and power chord shapes we have talked about so far. You can see that any given chord can be played in at least two different positions on the neck.

E Shapes

Major	Minor	Power

A Shapes

Major	Minor	Power

Fret	Major	Minor	Power	Major	Minor	Power
1	F	Fm	F5	A# or Bb	A#m or Bbm	A#5 or Bb5
2	F# or Gb	F#m or Gbm	F#5 or Gb5	B	Bm	B5
3	G	Gm	G5	C	Cm	C5
4	G# or Ab	G#m or Abm	G#5 or Ab5	C# or Db	C#m or Dbm	C#5 or Db5
5	A	Am	A5	D	Dm	D5
6	A# or Bb	A#m or Bbm	A#5 or Bb5	D# or Eb	D#m or Ebm	D#5 or Eb5
7	B	Bm	B5	E	Em	E5
8	C	Cm	C5	F	Fm	F5
9	C# or Db	C#m or Dbm	C#5 or Db5	F# or Gb	F#m or Gbm	F#5 or Gb5
10	D	Dm	D5	G	Gm	G5
11	D# or Eb	D#m or Ebm	D#5 or Eb5	G# or Ab	G#m or Abm	G#5 or Ab5
12	E	Em	E5	A	Am	A5

She Loves You

Where on the neck you play a chord may depend on where your left hand happens to be at the point in the song. A guitarist often goes to the nearest available voicing of the next chord. This is called **voice leading,** and tends to produce a smooth sounding progression from chord to chord. For example, if you are playing a **G** chord in third position (using an E shape bar chord) and the next chord is **B** minor, you would probably want to go the **B** minor at the second fret (the A minor shape) rather than the **B** minor at the seventh fret (the E minor shape), because it's closer.

The most effective rock guitar playing utilizes the two main bar-chord shapes, both major and minor, as well as open-position chords, riffs, and licks. All these elements are important to any given song, and the particular way a guitarist puts all these together reflects his style as well as his skill on the instrument. As you advance in your playing, you will be able to put these elements together more and more easily. Then your playing will begin to sound more "like the record." Instead of just strumming the chords to a song, you'll have the skills you'll need to play in a band.

With this in mind, let's start on our next song, the Beatles' "She Loves You." In this song we will use the two major chord shapes, the two minor chord shapes, some open chords, and some riffs.

"She Loves You" begins with eight measures of the chorus ("She loves you, yeah, yeah, yeah"). We are going to "voice lead" the chords in this section by using the shapes shown below for **Em, A7, C,** and **G.**

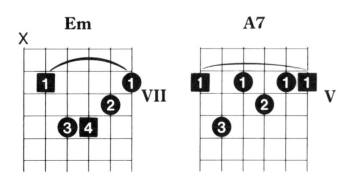

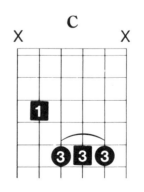

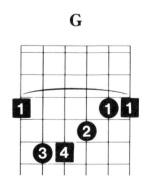

A7 is a new chord for you, but you can play it by fingering an E shape bar chord at the fifth fret and then lifting your fourth finger. Make sure that the note on the fourth string (that was covered by your fourth finger, but is now fretted by your first finger) is clearly heard. This is the note that makes the difference between an **A** chord and an **A7** chord. This seventh chord is a moveable shape. By lifting your fourth finger you can change any E shape bar chord to a seventh chord.

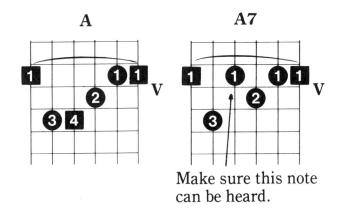

Make sure this note can be heard.

In the music below you can see the two-measure strumming pattern that we'll use for most of "She Loves You." In the first measure, simply play four quarter-notes. In the second measure, the second half of beat two (the "and" of two) is held over into beat three. Resume the strum on the "and" of three. Even though you don't play on beat three, your right hand should still be moving in a strict eighth-note pattern. On the held note (beat three), just lift the pick off the strings. Use this two-measure pattern throughout the song unless otherwise indicated. I've notated this one in the same key as the record, so if you have a copy you should be able to play right along.

She Loves You
Words and Music by John Lennon and Paul McCartney

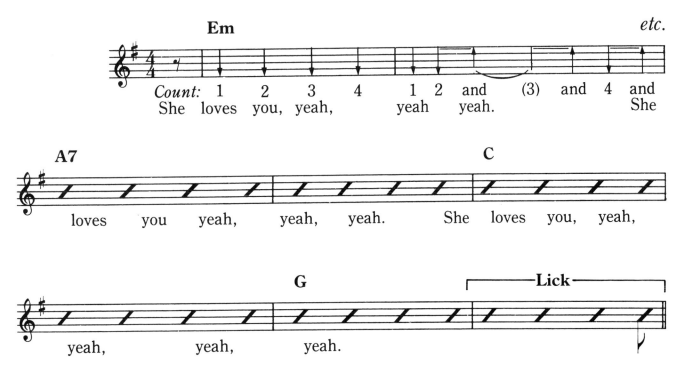

Above the last measure there is a line showing where George Harrison plays a lick that he uses several times in the song. Below, I've written out this lick, which is quite tasty and typical of his playing in the "early Beatles" period. Most of the notes come from the blues scale that we discussed in **Book 3**. Here the notes are played as **double stops.** Double stops are two-note chords.

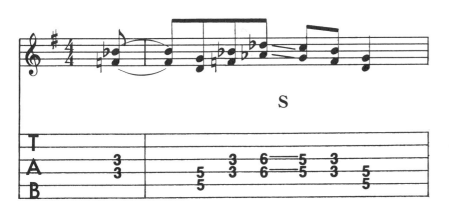

Finger this lick with your first finger covering the notes on the third fret and your third finger covering the notes on the fifth and sixth frets. There is a **slide** indicated between the notes on the sixth fret and the note on the fifth fret. To play this slide, finger the notes on the sixth fret, pick with your right hand, then slide the left-hand finger to the fifth fret, sounding the notes on this fret without picking again.

Now let's look at the chords for the rest of the song.

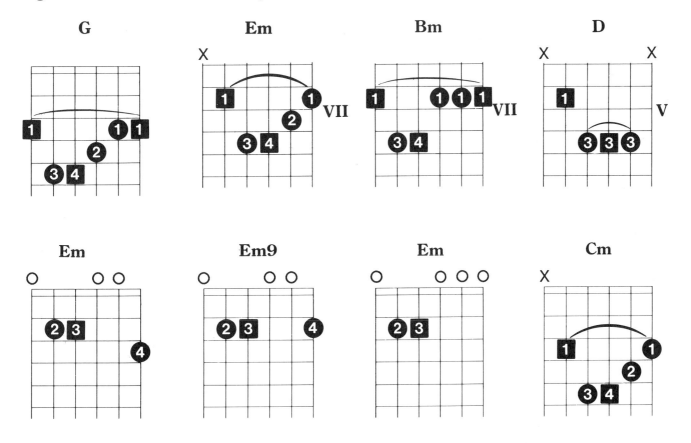

She Loves You *continued*

For the first eight measures of the verse we'll use the same strum that we used for the intro. In the eleventh and twelfth measures, we're going to use some special chord voicings to get the sound that you hear on the record after the words "and you know that can't be bad." These special voicings are the sequence of **Em** chords in the diagrams above that are played in open position. Notice that in this sequence the fourth finger moves from the third fret of the first string to the second fret of the first string (for the **Em9** chord) and then off, letting the open string sound. As you strum these three chords your ear hears the notes sounded on the high **E** string as a melody

because these are the highest notes of the voicings. This progression is indicated in notes and tablature in the music below. The entire verse is played twice (as shown by the repeat signs) but the lick that we learned for the intro is played only the first time. After playing the verse twice, go on to the chorus. Use the **Em** voicing at the seventh fret. The other chords are like those of the intro, except for the **Cm**. Also note that the strumming rhythm in the **Cm** bar has a rest on the fourth beat, after the words "love like that." At the end of the chorus the lick is heard again.

Verse

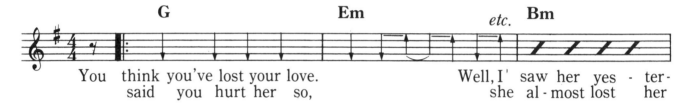

You think you've lost your love.
said you hurt her so,
Well, I' saw her yes - ter-
she al - most lost her

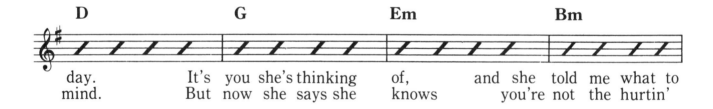

day.
mind.
It's you she's thinking of,
But now she says she knows
and she told me what to
you're not the hurtin'

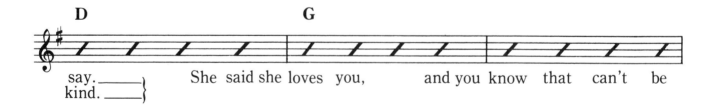

say.____ }
kind.____ }
She said she loves you, and you know that can't be

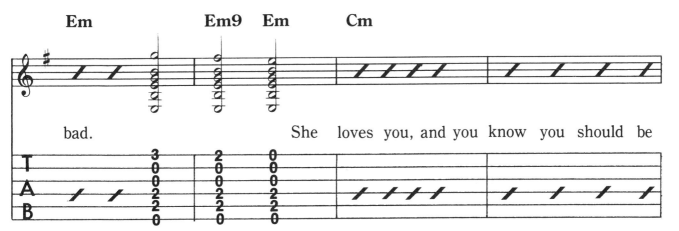

bad.   She loves you, and you know you should be

glad.   She glad.   She

Chorus

loves you, yeah,___yeah,_ yeah.   She loves you, yeah,_ yeah,_yeah. And with a

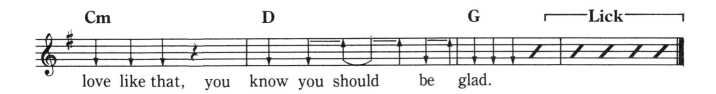

love like that,   you   know you should   be   glad.

More About Blues Scales

At the end of **Book 3** we saw how the notes of the blues scale could be used to make a solo which can be played against the chords of the twelve-bar blues progression. What we want to do now is expand this scale and see how it can be used to play against other chord progressions.

If you have already been experimenting with improvising guitar solos, you may have realized that certain scales and patterns seem to work best against certain chords. The question is, how do you know which scale to play against a given chord.

Answering this question can get complicated, but there are certain principles that are not hard to understand that will help you get started.

One important thing to realize is that the solos you hear on records are not random bunches of notes. If you've ever tried to figure out a solo from a record you may have become frustrated trying to follow the licks up and down the neck, not really knowing where to go next and wondering why the guitarist played the notes he did. But as you become more experienced, you begin to realize that most solos are made up of recognizable scales and patterns. If you know these patterns, figuring out solos (and taking your own solos) becomes much easier.

The main principle to keep in mind is that a scale goes with a **key.** A key represents a collection of notes and the chords that are made up of those notes. If you're jamming with some other musicians and you decide to play blues, someone will ask, "What key?" If you decide to play in the key of **A,** then you know that you can use the **A** blues scale to play lead and the chords of the **A** blues progression to play rhythm. More importantly, the chord **A** will be heard as "home," the area of resolution, and the note **A** will be heard as the "at rest" tone, the logical place to begin or end a melody line.

You do not have to change your scale every time a chord is changed, as long as the chords are all in the same key. For most rock guitar solos, one scale will see you through. What you do have to know is what key you're in.

Figuring out what key a certain song is in requires more music theory than we can go into here. However, if you use your ears and a little logical thinking it shouldn't be too difficult to figure out which chord and which tone are "home base." Frequently, the first and/or last chord of a song will represent the key of that song.

In **Book 3,** you learned that the blues scale (which is also called the **pentatonic minor** scale) looks like this:

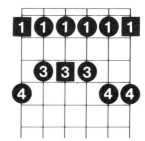

In the diagram above, the notes with squares around them are the roots of the scale. If you play this scale in third position, with the first note on the third fret of the low **E** string, you'll be playing a **G blues scale.** In seventh position you'll be playing a **B blues scale,** and in tenth position, a **D blues scale.** A scale can be moved around just like a chord, as long as no open strings are involved.

This blues scale is the scale that rock musicians use as their most basic tool for solos. Probably more than half of all the rock solos and riffs you have ever heard are based on this scale.

The chord progression below is one which is used in many songs and which is often used as the background for solos. This is the chord progression that Jimmy Page solos over in "Stairway to Heaven," and the one that Jimi Hendrix solos over in "All along the Watchtower."

Play this chord progression for a while to get used to the way it sounds. You can use the E minor shape bar chord in fifth position for the **Am** chord and the E shape bar chords in third and first positions for the **G** and **F** chords. What chord do you think is the **tonic** chord, the chord that is "home base"?

In this chord progression, the **Am** chord is the tonic chord. We could say that we are in the key of **A minor**, and that we'll use the **A** blues scale for soloing.

You already know one way to play the blues scale. I want to show you another place on the neck to play this scale to give you some more notes to work with. For the key of **A minor** (and, as we have seen, for blues in the key of **A**) you'll use the blues scale in fifth position. Let's call this **Pattern 1**. Below, I have diagrammed the same scale, but in a higher **register**. Let's call this **Pattern 2**. You can think of Pattern 2 as an extension of Pattern 1. The same scale is being used, but the notes are in a higher register, which means they are higher in pitch.

You can see from the diagram above that Pattern 2 starts on the fret where the fourth finger plays in Pattern 1. In **A**, Pattern 2 starts on the eighth fret, three frets higher than Pattern 1, which starts on the fifth fret. This relationship will be the same for any key. For example, in the key of **C**, Pattern 2 starts on the eleventh fret and Pattern 1 starts on the eighth fret. Notice that in Pattern 2 the root is played with the third finger on the second string.

Pattern 1   **Pattern 2**

Now let's return to our chord progression in **A minor**. The notes for the solo will be taken from the **A** blues scale, which we can play in two places on the neck. The notes in Pattern 1 and 2 look like this if we notate them on the staff and in tablature:

A Blues Scale
Pattern 1

Pattern 2

I'm going to show you some effects to give you some ideas for making up your own solos. In **Book 3** we talked about the 1/4 bend and vibrato. Another important effect in rock and blues soloing is the **whole-step bend.** To play a whole-step bend (which is also called simply a **bend**), finger a note and bend the string until you reach a new pitch that sounds a whole step (two frets) higher than the original pitch. In the bend below, use your third finger to play a **D** on the seventh fret of the third string. Now bend the string; that is, push the string up toward the **D** string. Your first, second, and third fingers should be lined up along the **G** string to help give you leverage. You want to bend the string until you hear the sound of the note that would be on the ninth fret of the third string. The **D** on the seventh fret is being bent to give you the sound of an **E**.

Notice that in the tablature the letter **B** indicates a bend. The note in parentheses represents the sound you are bending up to; the note before it is the note you finger.

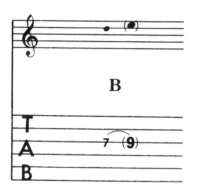

The whole-step bend is one of the most important devices that rock guitar players use to get that "major league" sound. In the diagrams below I've indicated the notes in Patterns 1 and 2 that are most often bent a whole step.

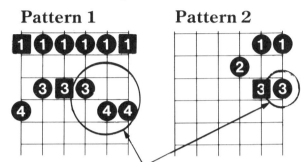

Pattern 1   **Pattern 2**

Most often bent a whole step.

Although Pattern 2 has only one commonly bent note, that bend is very effective. It will take some practice to get these bends down, but the results will be well worth your effort.

Another important effect is **vibrato.** There are several ways to execute a finger vibrato, but most rock guitar players play it by fingering a note and moving the left-hand finger up and down after the note is picked. (This movement is opposed to side-to-side, which is what is done by most classical players.) Vibrato causes the note to "waver" in pitch. This can be a great effect, but you must be careful that as you move the note up and down you return the string to its starting point each time. Otherwise you will cause the pitch to go sharp.

Every guitarist develops his vibrato and bend style as part of his individual sound. You can hear this by listening closely to such greats as Jimi Hendrix, B.B. King, Eric Clapton, Jimmy Page, and Jeff Beck. Listening to these players should give you some good ideas. All guitar players start out by copying their favorites on the way to getting their own sound. It's one of the most important ways of learning how to solo.

I've written out a solo (over the **Am-G-F** progression we looked at before) that uses notes from Pattern 1 and Pattern 2 and contains some bends and notes with vibrato.

Stairway to the Watchtower

Music by Steve Tarshis

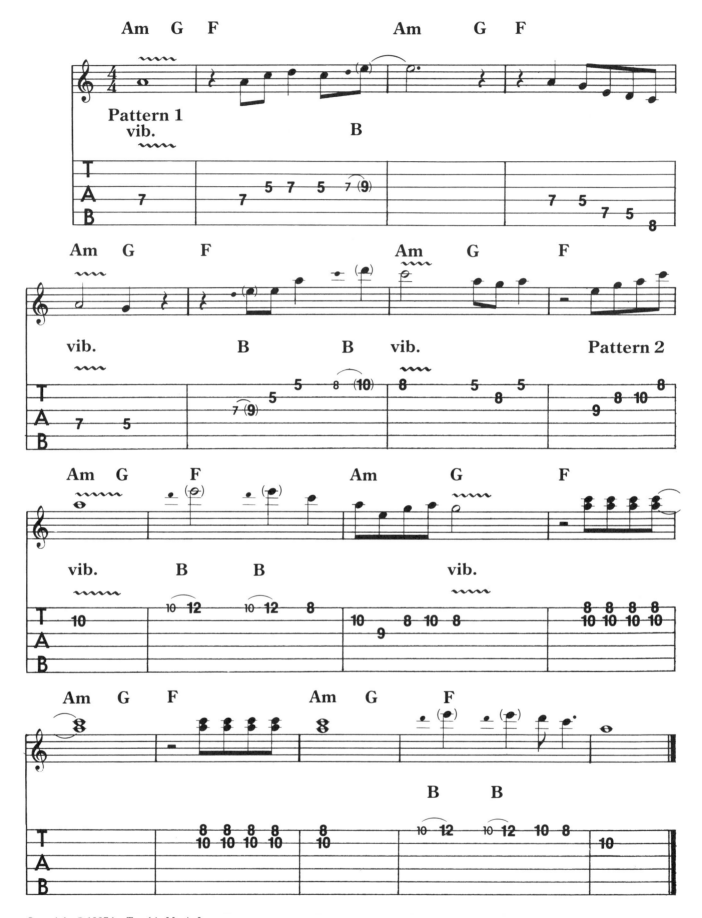

Closing Comments

This brings us to the close of the **Complete Rock Guitar Player** series. I hope that you have had fun along the way and that you are satisfied with how far you have come as a rock guitar player. Keep practicing all of the chords, scales, techniques, and progressions you have learned, because the material we've covered in these four books is a solid foundation that can enable you to build your own, truly personal rock style. Don't forget to keep your ears (and your mind) open when listening to other rock guitar players — you now have the tools to understand and apply a lot of what you hear.